Chicken In The Car And The Car Won't Go

Nearly 200 Ways to Enjoy Chicagoland with Tweens and Teens

Chicken In The Car And The Car Won't Go

Nearly 200 Ways to Enjoy Chicagoland with Tweens and Teens

For the Patton family!
Have Fun!

Melisa Wells

Melisa Wells

♡

LITTLE CREEK BOOKS

A division of Mountain Girl Press
Bristol, VA

LITTLE CREEK BOOKS

A division of Mountain Girl Press
Bristol, VA

CHICKEN IN THE CAR AND THE CAR WON'T GO:

Nearly 200 Ways to Enjoy Chicagoland with Tweens and Teens

You may contact the publisher at:
Little Creek Books
A Division of Mountain Girl Press
2195 Euclid Avenue, Suite 7
Bristol, VA 24201
E-mail: publisher@littlecreekbooks.com

ISBN: 978-0-9846398-1-6

Contents

Acknowledgments

This book is a labor of love that has percolated for much longer than the six years I have actively worked on it, because I was born with a piece of my heart already dedicated to the great city of Chicago! Thanks to my parents for treating me to adventures like watching the light shows at Buckingham Fountain, shopping at Marshall Field's on State Street, strolling up and down Michigan Avenue, touring the Coal Mine at the Museum of Science and Industry, and gazing at the corn cob-like towers of Marina City, the home of my dreams since those early days. It's their fault I love this city as much as I do.

I am very blessed to have many loving and supportive friends in my life. I can't list the names of each and every one of them, but must thank a representative few who gave me extra strength and encouragement during this process. Liz Thompson, Diane Lang, Carol Cain, Melanie Salyers, and John Cave Osborne were really good at calming me down, helping me make decisions, giving me great advice, and—always—making me laugh.

Michelle Price was a tremendous resource for me in the writing and publishing of this book, definitely much more than she'll ever know. She played many parts along the way including fact-checker, editor, cheerleader, advisor, and most of all, good friend.

Many, many thanks to Tammy Robinson Smith at Little Creek Books, whose expertise (and humor!) was invaluable in making this dream come true.

My sister Julie is one of my biggest supporters and a featured player in many of my favorite Chicago adventures. Much love and thanks to her for the photo session that resulted in the fabulous author picture, for the hours she spent editing (and re-editing) my manuscript, and for consulting with the cover artist over details I can't begin to understand. Her contributions, as they always are no matter what the project, were above and beyond.

There aren't enough words to express the love and appreciation I have for my husband. Jim doesn't care for the hustle and bustle of the city, traffic, flat landscapes, and extreme winters one bit, yet he puts up with all of it because he married a Chicago girl. He has been my number one source of love and encouragement, and I couldn't have reached this point without him and his steadfast support.

Lastly, thanks to the two reasons I wrote this particular book in the first place, my awesome sons Dylan and Jason. They are always willing sidekicks who show up with smiling faces. The Fun and memories we have created together over the years will be in my heart forever and ever.

Melisa Wells

Introduction

Let's get something out of the way: I'll bet you're wondering about the silly title of this book, aren't you? It comes from some verse that my mom used to recite constantly when I was a kid:

> *"Chicken in the car and the car won't go*
> *That's the way to spell Chicago.*
> *A knife and a fork! A bottle and a cork!*
> *That's the way to spell New York."*

I always thought the verse was very whimsical, and it stuck with me. I never imagined I would have much use for it; little did I know that it would become part of the memories I made with my own children as they approached those ominous tween and teen years.

Many parents dread the ages of eleven to nineteen, otherwise known as the tweens and teens. And why wouldn't they? The media goes on and on about how hard it is to get along with kids at this age. As teenagers struggle to walk the developmental line between child and adult, what they really need is the support of their family. Parents who make the extra effort to communicate, spend time, and really relate with their tweens and teens are doing everyone a favor. Rather than dread, I chose early on to embrace, and part of that plan included sharing some of the Chicago traditions that my own parents started with me when I was a youngster.

As children of Chicago natives growing up in the south suburbs, my sister and I experienced what the city offered on a regular basis. It wasn't unusual for us to drive into the city (or take the train) just to see a show, visit a museum, or enjoy a great meal; it was a part of life.

Our parents also exposed us to great 1970s fun in suburbia, like the no longer existent "Old Chicago" Shopping Center and Amusement Park in Bolingbrook. We visited Six Flags Great America in Gurnee during its first season, when it was known as Marriott's Great America. We even found fun over the border, like Honey Bear Farm in Powers Lake, Wisconsin, which has—unfortunately—been closed for more than twenty-five years. My Chicago-area childhood memory bank also includes activities like blueberry picking, flea markets, and behind-the-scenes tours.

We moved away when I was nine, and after years of living in several other United States cities, I finally returned "home" in 1995 when my husband Jim and I settled in the western suburbs of Chicago. As luck would have it, Naperville, Illinois has been on some great lists in the past several years, including "The Best Place to Live" and "The Best Place to Raise Children." Park District programming in this area is absolutely fantastic, and there is a lot to do . . . but most of the best-known activities and places to visit are for kids about ten and younger. When I checked into the available Chicago travel guides, I found the same: most of the information was geared towards families with young children. What about tweens and teens? I was certain that there was age-appropriate fun for my older kids *somewhere*; I just had to dig a little deeper to find it!

I spent many hours during my kids' summer breaks from school trying to discover activities that Jim and I could enjoy with them. For a few years, we structured the assortment of things to do like our own summer camp (there is more about how to plan one for your family on page 211), and we spent many days exploring the Chicago area in bite-sized pieces. After a while, Jim mentioned that he thought I had enough information to fill a book, and the rest is history.

Most people don't take the time to enjoy the fun that is indigenous to their local area because it's always . . . there. They consume energy and money on vacations that are a car, train, or plane ride away in order to explore what they don't have in their own backyard. At least that's how it used to be. With the unstable economy of the past few years, there is a greater emphasis on "staycations." Simplified, a staycation is the enjoyment of what's available close to home. Anytime is a great time to become a local expert!

On the following pages you will find the results of my extensive research. It is my strongest hope that you will use it often to make some forever memories with your own kids. From my family to yours, enjoy!

Melisa Wells
April 2011

For Dylan and Jason, my favorite teens in the whole world.

Part One

Navigation

How To Use This Book

As you begin planning your own family adventures, please take into consideration what I've learned from trial and error. In other words, feel free to benefit from my personal disasters, of which there have been many. First and foremost, even though all information listed was correct at press time, make sure before leaving the house for a planned attraction or activity that the hours haven't changed and even that the place is still open for business. There were times my family and I spent hours in the car going from closed place to closed place because I didn't double-check business hours before pulling out of the driveway. I don't make that mistake anymore.

Secondly, while not every activity listed in these pages is going to please everyone, it helps to keep an open mind. Discovering unique, local treasures at places like the Lizzadro Museum of Lapidary Art (Elmhurst), the International Museum of Surgical Science (Chicago), or the Skokie Northshore Sculpture Park (of course, Skokie) won't happen if your idea of Fun (with a capital F) is limited to places that are familiar. I included a wide variety of destinations within these pages, because as my mom always said, one man's trash is another man's treasure. And really, what's wrong with trying something that's outside of the comfort zone? (Nothing.)

Rather than exact pricing, symbols are used throughout the book to provide a *general* idea of cost. Because in so many cases a teenager's admission costs the same as an adult's, the symbol will reflect the average cost per person.

♦ = Variable pricing (*Example: shopping*)

✪ = FREE

$ = $5 or less

$$ = $6–10

$$$ = $11–15

$$$$ = $16–25

$$$$$ = $26 and up

Though high prices are typical at professional sporting events or shows, the activities in this book run the gamut where pricing is concerned. Believe it or not, there is still free fun to be had in the Chicago area! I recommend checking current prices before hitting the road. Let the buyer beware: although it seems logical that a company's website would always contain the most accurate information, the level of website upkeep varies from place to place. If I absolutely need firm information, I always pick up the phone.

The description on each destination includes a "*Tweens and Teens Tip,*" which is something that this age group might find particularly interesting about the activity, something special offered to tweens and teens exclusively, or just a little known fact about the place that might enhance an experience there.

Attractions and activities in this book are grouped by city and suburban area, for ease in planning geographically. For those whose fun-seeking efforts know no boundaries, I have included three indexes: alphabetical order, by activity name, and by city.

Finally, remember that the idea here is to have Fun (with a capital F) together as a family. If big Fun is planned for the afternoon but the kids are bickering all morning, it's probably a good idea to restructure the day's game plan. Going into a family activity with participants who are already emotionally spent will definitely have an adverse effect on the day and the memory of it. I have temporarily disappointed all of us by canceling a daytrip or two, but when we rescheduled, we had a much better time than we originally would have.

Well, why wait any longer? *Get going!*

Getting Around, Staying Informed, and Other Helpful Tips

The Chicago area is huge. Just getting from the Loop to Wrigley Field or U.S. Cellular Field can take a while when traffic or construction reroutes are thrown into the mix. Traveling from the city to the suburbs and back requires a little bit of planning. Fortunately many transportation options are available when it comes to getting around.

Travel by car

Driving — though not always the fastest way to get from point A to point B — is the best way to get around in the suburban areas surrounding the city. Becoming familiar with the highway system is a good idea, and a GPS doesn't hurt either.

The main north-south arteries are the Tri-State Tollway (I-94/I-294/I-80) and the Veterans Memorial Tollway (I-355) in the suburbs. (Note that I-94 is an east/west interstate highway that happens to run north/south as it passes through the state of Illinois.) The highways that radiate out from the city are the Jane Addams Memorial Tollway (I-90) to the northwest, the Eisenhower Expressway (I-290) and the Reagan Memorial Tollway (I-88) to the west, and the Stevenson Expressway (I-55) to the south. When watching or listening to a traffic report, it is important to know that sections of highway are mostly referred to by names instead of by number.

The major highways (and their names) in the Chicago area are as follows:

- **Tri-State Tollway** (I-94/I-294/I-80): Extends from just west of the Indiana state line where it intersects with the Bishop Ford and the Kingery Expressways to a point near the Illinois-Wisconsin border, where it connects with U.S. Route 41 and U.S. Interstate Highway 94 from Milwaukee.

- **Kennedy Expressway** (I-90 & I-94): Extends from downtown Chicago, northwest to River Road near O'Hare International Airport (I-190 runs from the end of the Kennedy, west and directly into O'Hare).

- **Jane Addams Memorial Tollway** (I-90): Begins east of the interchange with the Kennedy and the Tri-State Tollway and extends west, crossing the Fox River just north of Elgin, Illinois. From there, it runs northwest towards Rockford and then north to just south of the Wisconsin state border.

- **Edens Expressway** (I-94 & U.S. Route 41): Stretches from the interchange with the Kennedy Expressway near Montrose, north to the Lake County line near Northbrook. The Edens Spur (I-94) travels west, connecting the Edens to the Tri-State Tollway.

- **Dan Ryan** (I-90 & I-94): Extends south from the Circle Interchange (where the Kennedy, Eisenhower, & Congress Parkway meet) to the Bishop Ford Freeway (I-94). The Bishop Ford continues south and east to I-80 near the Indiana state border.

- **Eisenhower Expressway** (I-290): Runs from the Circle Interchange west through the suburbs and interchanging with the Reagan Memorial Tollway (I-88), on to the west. It then migrates to the north and ends near Woodfield Mall in Schaumburg at the Jane Addams Memorial Tollway (I-90) interchange.

- **Reagan Memorial Tollway** (I-88): Begins east of the junction of the Tri-State Tollway and the Eisenhower Expressway and runs southwest and west past Dixon, Illinois (hometown of Ronald Reagan), to U.S. Route 30 in the Sterling/Rock Falls area.

- **Veterans Memorial Tollway** (I-355): Runs north/south from I-290 in Itasca (Army Trail Road) to I-80 in New Lenox.

The quickest — and cheapest — way for locals and frequent visitors to travel on the tollway is by using I-PASS, which is an electronic toll collection system from the Illinois Tollway. Transponders can be purchased at an Illinois Tollway office or one of the I-PASS partner locations, which can be found by searching the IDOT website (www .illinoistollway.com). I-PASS is part of the EZ-Pass consortium, which means it can be used in fourteen states: Illinois, Indiana, Ohio, Pennsylvania, West Virginia, Virginia, Maryland, Delaware, New Jersey, New York, Rhode Island, Massachusetts, New Hampshire, and Maine. The benefits to using I-PASS are the elimination of the need to carry change for tolls, access to the open road toll lanes (which eliminates the need for coming to a complete stop at a tollbooth), and the cost of the toll itself: paying cash instead of using I-PASS doubles the toll cost.

The Illinois Tollway offers a seven-day grace period to drivers who miss paying a toll. Make sure to jot down which tolls were missed because the Illinois Tollway needs that information in order to process payments, which can be made online or by mail. If the toll is not paid within the seven days, it becomes a violation and is subject to associated fines in addition to the tolls.

Because traffic is one of the daily elements of life in Chicagoland, the local news stations (both television and radio) are well versed in letting drivers know which areas to avoid, and updates are frequent during the morning and evening rush hours.

Parking a car in the city can be an expensive proposition. Though some garages and lots have "early bird specials," the start time on these is usually more commuter-friendly rather than tourist-friendly. When parking a car for more than a couple of hours because of a visit to a

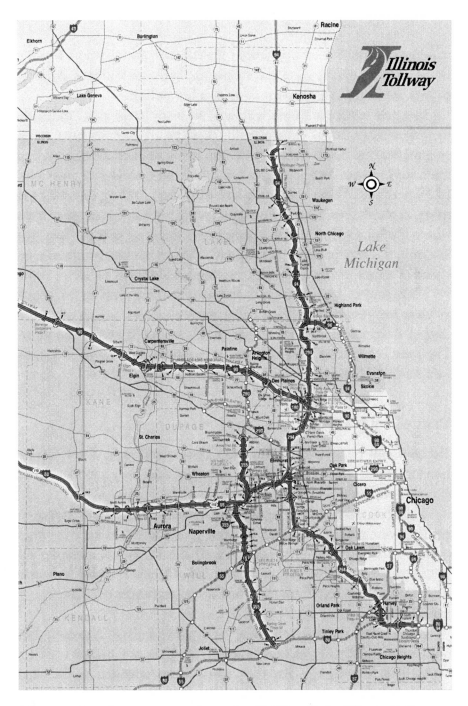

Map used with permission from the IDOT and the Illinois Tollway.

9

museum or other attraction, check for available parking before leaving home. Many places — retail stores included — validate parking tickets, resulting in a discount of up to a few dollars.

Metered street parking is available in many areas and, compared to garage prices, is less expensive for short visits. At press time, Loop area meters cost $5.00 per hour, central business district (surrounding the Loop) meters cost $3.00 per hour, and most other city areas cost $1.50 per hour. There is a two-hour limit when parking in a metered space. A meter receipt can be used for parking in a different space from where it originated as long as that space is the same cost per hour (or less) and the receipt hasn't yet expired. Visit www.chicagometers.com ahead of time to scope out street parking possibilities.

Make sure to pay attention to signs and parking restrictions. Many a driver has returned to his parking space to find a ticket, or in the case of a serious infraction, no car at all because it was towed away. The location of towed vehicles can be found on the City of Chicago's website (http://findyourvehicle.cityofchicago.org).

Travel by Taxicab

Taxicabs can be found all over the Chicagoland area. They can be hired for quick trips of a few blocks or longer rides, for example, to the airport from the city or any suburb.

Riding in a cab is fairly reasonable in *most* cases. (When trying to get from one end of Michigan Avenue to the other at certain times of day, walking might be a better idea.) An initial charge is levied just for getting into the cab, and every 1/8 of a mile traveled increases it. A surcharge is levied for each additional passenger over the age of twelve and under the age of sixty-five.

Car seat use for children under eight years old is only required in non-commercial vehicles (according to the City of Chicago website: www.cityofchicago.org), but their use is recommended in Chicago taxicabs for children who weigh less than fifty pounds. Occasionally a cab driver may store a child safety seat in the trunk for his customers' use, but to ensure the same level of protection as at home, bring one along.

Travel by Bus

The 140-route bus system, run by the Chicago Transit Authority (CTA), is an excellent way to get around the city. Route maps and other information are available on the CTA website (www.transitchicago.com). Generally, buses arrive every fifteen to twenty minutes. Make sure that the bus you plan to take has the correct route number displayed on the illuminated sign above the windshield; the driver can also verify the destination.

Buses accept fare payments of cash, fare cards (Chicago Card, Chicago Card Plus, and Transit Cards), and passes, which allow unlimited rides for a specific time. A complete guide to fares, as well as eligibility requirements for reduced rides, is found on the CTA website.

The CTA offers a program through which riders can get estimated arrival times by text. Usage instructions and tips for the Bus Tracker can be found online as well as on a growing number of bus stop signs.

Suburban riders are served by Pace, a sister agency of the CTA. Information about fares, routes, and CTA connections can be found on the Pace website (www.pacebus.com).

Travel by Train

The Chicago area is served by two different rail systems, Metra and the "L." Eleven Metra lines transport passengers between the four stations in the loop and outposts in the six-county Northern Illinois area, plus the Kenosha, Wisconsin station on the Union Pacific North line. The Metra fare system is distance-based with twelve zones on each line. Fares are determined according to how many zones are traveled through.

Metra train schedules can be found online (www.metrarail.com) and vary according to weekday, Saturday, or Sunday. In addition to one-way tickets, Metra also offers 10-ride tickets, monthly tickets, and unlimited weekend passes. Discounts are offered for children, families, students, seniors, and disabled riders. Ticket purchases can be made online, by mail, at the station, and on the train. A word of caution: a service fee will be imposed on tickets purchased from the conductor on the train if a ticket agent is on duty at the station of departure.

As one would expect, the trains are more crowded during commuting hours; however, early morning and early evening are also the times of day when more express trains are offered. Express trains make very few stops and can shave a substantial amount of time off of the ride. It is advisable to double-check the scheduled stops before boarding, because each express route varies.

For city plans that last into the wee hours, be advised that the latest Metra trains depart the city between midnight and 1:00 a.m. on the major lines.

The "L," or *elevated train rapid transit system*, is operated by the CTA. Oddly enough, only part of the system is actually elevated; the rest of it runs at street level and below ground. Eight lines (Red, Blue, Brown, Green, Orange, Purple, Pink, and Yellow) serve 144 stations throughout the city and suburbs, including the O'Hare airport station at the end of the Blue Line, and the Orange Line station at Midway Airport.

The fare for riding the "L" is payable with the Chicago Card, Chicago Card Plus, or transit cards; cash is not accepted. Cards can be purchased at all train stations and other locations in the city which are listed on the CTA website (www.transitchicago.com). Helpful travel tools also found on the website include applications (apps) for mobile phones and desktop computers and a downloadable Downtown Transit Sightseeing Guide which can be printed.

Alternate Methods

For a different (and relatively quick) way to get around the city, the Chicago Water Taxi is perfect. Running on the Chicago River from

Michigan Avenue at the base of the Wrigley Building to Chinatown at Ping Tom Memorial Park, the water taxis also stop between LaSalle and Clark Streets at Fulton Market and at Madison Street, across the river from the Civic Opera House. Single rides can be purchased, as can All Day, Ten Ride, and Monthly Unlimited passes. More information, including schedules, can be found on the official website (www .chicagowatertaxi.com).

Over the last decade, Chicago has gained a reputation for being extremely bicycle-friendly. With the active and public support of the Mayor's office, the Chicago Department of Transportation's Bike Program aims to promote this practical, environmentally friendly, and affordable method of transport. Most city streets can be traversed (carefully), and there are plenty of trails (including the popular Lakefront Trail) on which to ride. More information about the city's bike initiatives, including a bike rack search, are available online (www.chicagobikes.org).

In the suburbs, hundreds of miles of trails are available for bicycle use. Forest preserves and parks are plentiful. The Illinois Prairie Path (located mostly in DuPage County) and the North Shore Channel Trail (located in Cook County) are only two examples of the extensive trail systems located throughout Chicagoland. Information and maps for more than forty area trails can be found at the Chicago Bike Trails website (www.chicagobiketrails.net.).

CTA and Pace buses are fitted with bicycle racks that carry two bicycles each. Passengers on the "L" and on Metra trains are allowed to bring bicycles on board with them during select times. Check each company's website for more information.

Weather

Discussing the weather — the good, bad, and the ugly — is a favorite pastime for Chicago natives. The area is famous for brutal winters, but there are more frigid places to be in the middle of January. Though sometimes it seems like summer ends and winter begins (and vice versa) with no buffer season in between, Chicago's four seasons are mostly distinct. "Construction," by the way, counts for many Chicagoans as a fifth season!

The best times of year to visit are from the beginning of May until early June and from the middle of September into October. During the extremely hot summers, humidity is a frequent problem. In the middle of the city, the temperatures can be practically unbearable due to the absorption of heat by the buildings, but relief can be found near the lake. The infamous Chicago winters are bitterly cold with harsh winds and an average of thirty-eight inches of snowfall each year. (Contrary to popular belief, major, city-closing blizzards occur only every two to three years.)

Chicagoland's driest months are January and February; the most precipitation falls in May, July, and August. Average temperatures in the summer range between 78–90, and average temperatures in the winter range between 25–32.

When packing for a Chicago trip, it's best to consider dressing in layers. The weather is often different from minute to minute, and the ability to remove and replace items of clothing can enhance comfort and enjoyment of every adventure.

Television Stations

The Chicago area has no shortage of entertaining and informative local television stations From the "Big Three" to WGN-9, which is a part of most cable packages nationwide, to the strong PBS station, to the independents, there is always something to watch. Here is a partial list of local television stations:

2   WBBM (CBS 2)

5   WMAQ (NBC 5)

7   WLS (ABC 7)

9   WGN (The CW)

11   WTTW (PBS)

23   WWME (Me TV)

26   WCIU (The U)

32   WFLD (Fox)

44   WSNS (Telemundo Chicago)

50   WPWR (My 50)

Radio Stations

Chicago is the 3rd largest radio market according to Arbitron (a media and marketing research firm), placing behind New York and LA. Generally speaking, there's something for everyone. Here is a partial list of local radio stations:

FM

92.3   WPWX (Power 92)

93.1   WXRT (Chicago's Finest Rock)

93.9   WLIT (The Lite)

94.7   WLS (Chicago's True Oldies Channel)

95.5   WNUA (Latin Pop)

95.9   WERV (The River)

96.3   WBBM (B-96)

97.1   WDRV (The Drive)

97.9   WLUP (The Loop)

98.7   WFMT (Chicago's Fine Arts Station)

99.5   WUSN (US99 America's Country)

100.3   WILV (LOVEfm)

101.1   WKQX (The Alternative Q101)

101.9   WTMX (The Mix)

102.7   WVAZ (Today's R&B and Old School V103)

103.5   WKSC (103.5 KISS FM)

104.3   WJMK (K-HITS)

105.1   WOJO (La Que Buena 105.1)

105.9   WCKG (Fresh 105.9)

107.5   WGCI (107.5 #1 For Hip Hop & R&B)

107.9   WLEY (La Ley 107.9)

AM

560   WIND (Conservative Talk)

670   WSCR (The Score Sports Radio)

720   WGN (News/Talk 720)

780   WBBM (Newsradio 780)

890   WLS (Newstalk 890)

1300   WRDZ (Radio Disney)

Newspapers and Magazines

There are plenty of publications that can provide information from around the globe to local news and activities. Here is a partial list of local newspapers:

Chicago Reader — alternative newspaper covering city news, events, and issues

Chicago Sun-Times — daily newspaper covering world, national, and local news

Chicago Tribune — major newspaper covering world, national, and local news

Crain's Chicago Business — news in business and finance

Pioneer Press — covers many Chicago suburbs, mainly in the north

SouthtownStar — covers the South Side of the city and the south suburbs

Suburban Chicago Newspapers — covers western suburbs

Here is a partial list of local magazines:

Chicago Magazine — lifestyle, human interest, travel, entertainment

Chicago Parent — geared towards families with younger children

Chicago Parent Going Places — family-friendly activities in Chicago and beyond

Concierge Preferred Magazine — shopping and restaurants

Glancer Magazine — shopping and events in the western suburbs

Suburban Focus Magazine — lifestyle, fitness, travel, family activities in the suburbs

Key Magazine — family activities

Time Out Chicago — events, dining, and things to do

West Suburban Living — local trends, shopping, and activities in the western suburbs

Visitor Information Centers

The city of Chicago has two visitor information centers staffed by Chicago experts who can help with an itinerary, suggest a great place to eat, or find information on special events. The centers also house a wealth of brochures, maps, and coupons.

Chicago Water Works Visitor Information Center
163 E. Pearson Street
(At Michigan Avenue and Pearson Street, across from Water Tower Place)

Chicago Cultural Center Visitor Information Center
77 E. Randolph Street
(At Michigan Avenue and Randolph Street, just north of Millennium Park)

The operating hours for both centers are:
Monday–Thursday 8:00 a.m.–7:00 p.m.
Friday 8:00 a.m.–6:00 p.m.
Saturday 9:00 a.m.–6:00 p.m.
Sunday 10:00 a.m.–6:00 p.m.
Holidays 10:00 a.m.–4:00 p.m.

The visitor information centers are closed on Thanksgiving, Christmas Day, and New Year's Day.

Travel counselors are available by phone from 8:00 a.m. until 7:00 p.m. daily at 1-877-CHICAGO (244-2246). On Twitter (see page 19), the Chicago Office of Tourism's handle is @explorechicago.

Social Media

As part of 21st century living, companies everywhere are taking the leap into social media on the internet in order to better connect with their customers. Using Facebook and Twitter for online marketing is one way that savvy businesses are getting the word out these days. As a customer, connecting via social media can sometimes result in rewards like up-to-the-minute information or special discounts.

Facebook used to be known as the website through which high school and college friends reconnect, but that has changed somewhat. Fan pages are a huge part of the phenomenon, and they're easy to find by using the search feature. By creating a page, a business can provide updates on operations or hours, directions, photos, and much more, all on a website that is separate from their external home page, with a more accessible feeling to some users. Updates and changes can be made on a Facebook page instantaneously and as often as the administrator desires.

What could the advantage be, of "liking," or signing up with, a business' Facebook page, rather than just visiting their main web page? It's simple: everyone who "likes" (or "fans") a business gets updates from that company in the news feed. This is a great way to keep an eye out for special pricing or alerts that their webmaster wouldn't necessarily put on their main website. The best part is, the news comes looking for customers instead of the other way around.

The impact of Twitter has been felt around the world, especially over the past year. Twitter is a micro-blogging website through which users can "tweet" status updates that are 140 characters or less, to other users who "follow" them. Initially, updates were intended to answer the question *What are you doing?* but users began adding conversations with others — at 140 characters or less, per tweet — that caused Twitter to change the question to *What's happening?* and the service morphed into a combination of blogging and instant messaging.

The very mention of Twitter can cause passionate responses in people: most either love it or hate it. It can be advantageous for travelers to sign up for an account and follow the businesses that will be experienced during the course of their adventures. Like Facebook, Twitter can be a great source for news and discounts. Twitter updates that go directly to a mobile phone can be set up on an individual basis, business by business, with just one click. By doing this, it is possible to get a question answered by sending a tweet to a business from a cell phone. When they reply, it will come straight back to that phone, no internet connection needed. (Settings can be changed anytime and as frequently as desired.) Some businesses will, on occasion, send out a special offer via Twitter. Some businesses, like regular people, are more active than others, and if a company's latest Twitter update is not in the recent past, a phone call might be a better choice when in need of immediate information.

The listings in this book include the Twitter handles of all businesses that have them, and were current as of press time.

Part Two
The Places

Chicago Loop

As you will notice by the sheer number of places included this section, the Loop is where you can get more "bang for your buck" when it comes to number of activities per square mile. The images of the Loop are also what comes to mind for most people when they think of Chicago. The geographical borders of the Loop area are the Chicago River on the west and north, Lake Michigan on the east, and Congress Parkway on the south. This is where you'll find the shopping and theater districts as well as government offices both for Chicago and Cook County. The Loop is colorful, vibrant, noisy, full of people and great for exploring.

A special note: Museum Campus seems to be in a category all its own. Technically it is part of the south side (it's on the northern edge!), but many people, tourists and locals alike, consider it to be a part of the Loop. For that reason, the attractions of Museum Campus (the Adler Planetarium, the Field Museum, and the Shedd Aquarium) are included in this section.

Adler Planetarium

1300 S. Lake Shore Drive
Chicago
312-922-7827
www.adlerplanetarium.org
$$–$$$$
Hours: Mon–Fri 10:00 a.m.–4:00 p.m., Sat–Sun 10:00 a.m.–4:30 p.m.
Twitter: @adlerskywatch

America's first planetarium, the Adler has been a part of Chicago since 1930. Its domed silhouette makes it one of the Windy City's most recognizable buildings. Home to three full sized theaters and exhibits about everything in the universe, the Adler Planetarium's mission is to inspire visitors to learn more about science and space.

Exhibits include "Our Solar System," "From the Night Sky to the Big Bang," and "Universe in Your Hands," all of which contain interactive elements to make a visit more enjoyable. General Admission includes exhibits only. Other admission options are available for those who wish to see a show and experience a guided tour of the Atwood Sphere, which is a virtual tour of the night sky over Chicago as it appeared in 1913.

Tweens and Teens Tip: Because the Adler Planetarium is on the easternmost tip of Northerly Island, make sure to take in the view before you leave the area. Take a water taxi from Museum Campus to Navy Pier for a view like no other.

Bike and Roll Chicago

Starting Point Varies
Chicago
(312) 729-1000
www.bikechicago.com
$$$$
Hours: Vary. Equipment rental and tours are seasonal.
Check the website for details.
Twitter: @bike_chicago

Exploring Chicago from a four-wheeled vehicle limits your view and ability to access certain areas that are best seen up close. Bike Chicago offers guided tours and, if you're in the mood for guiding yourself around the city, also rents bicycles, inline skates, and Segways by the hour, half-day, and full-day.

Tours offered include the *Chicago River & Parks Tour, Bikes@Nite Tour, Amazing Lakefront Tour, Friendly Neighborhoods Tour*, and the *Presidential Bike Tour*, which takes riders by President and Michelle Obama's Hyde Park home as well as other sites integral to Obama's time in Chicago. Each tour is two to three hours long and rated an "easy ride" by the operator (bikes are included). Reservations are highly recommended for tours and equipment rentals.

Tweens and Teens Tip: Bike Chicago has locations scattered all over the city for convenience and variety. You can get your ride on from Millennium Park, Navy Pier, Riverwalk, North Avenue Beach, the DuSable Museum of African American History, the Adler Planetarium, and the Oak Street, Ohio Street, or Foster Beaches. Participants under the age of eighteen are required to wear a helmet, which is free with rental.

Chicago Architecture Foundation Tours

Starting Point Varies
Chicago
(312) 922-3432
www.architecture.org
$$$–$$$$
Hours: Vary. Check the website for details.
Twitter: @chiarchitecture

If you're looking for an excellent tour of Chicago, check out the Chicago Architecture Foundation (CAF) website. The Foundation has given tourists and locals an inside view of the city since the late sixties, and in so many ways: tours are currently offered by boat, bus, bike, Segway, and on foot. Their *Architectural Boat Tour*, a 90-minute journey during which a CAF-certified docent shares facts about the design, history, and current tenants of many world-class buildings along the Chicago River, is Chicago's most popular river cruise.

Other CAF tours include neighborhoods, churches, skyscrapers, parks, sculpture, and even a look at the "Bungalow Belt." The yearly tour directory, complete with tour descriptions, pricing, and availability, can be found on the website.

Tweens and Teens Tip: Advance ticket purchase is highly recommended, especially for the *Architectural Boat Tour*. CAF docent Geoffrey Baer periodically hosts tours for programs on WTTW-11, which are always nice to watch from the comfort of home. However, to truly experience the city and its spectacular architecture, get off the couch and enjoy a close-up view. For more boat tours of Chicago, see "Touring Chicagoland," which begins on page 189.

Chicago Chocolate Tours

Starting Points Vary
Chicago
312-929-2939
www.chicagochocolatetours.com
$$$$$
Hours: Vary. Check the website for details.
Twitter: @chichoctours

Chicago Chocolate Tours' founder Valerie Beck and her team of "Choc Stars," tour guides who are trained to lead groups directly to the finest chocolate in the city, give the most gastronomically decadent tours of Chicago. Tour participants learn about fine chocolates, the history of chocolate, and tidbits about the architecture of Chicago along the way.

Many different tours are available, covering manageable slices of the city's chocolate landscape: the South Loop, the Loop, the Downtown Loop, Lincoln Park, Lakeview, and the Magnificent Mile/Gold Coast area. Tours are on foot and last for approximately two and a half hours. Reservations are required.

Tweens and Teens Tip: When booking, pay attention to the walking levels, which range from easy to intermediate. If you take the *Downtown Loop* tour, check out Master Chocolatier Joseph Schmidt's Chicago skyline made of chocolate, which is located at Macy's on State Street.

Museum

Chicago Cultural Center

78 E. Washington Street

Chicago

(312) 744-6630

www.chicagoculturalcenter.org

✪

Hours: Mon–Thurs 8:00 a.m.–7:00 p.m., Fri 8:00 a.m.–6:00 p.m.,
Sat 9:00 a.m.–6:00 p.m., Sun 10:00 a.m.–6:00 p.m. Closed holidays.
Twitter: @explorechicago

Originally Chicago's first central public library, the Chicago Cultural Center is a Chicago Landmark located two blocks north of the Art Institute. It was built in 1897 from exquisite glass, marble and stone to show the world Chicago's sense of modern elegance. It is home to the world's largest stained glass Tiffany dome—containing more than 30,000 pieces of glass—as well as a second dome designed by Healy and Millet. Free building tours are offered many times throughout the week.

In addition to the beauty of the building, visitors can enjoy more than one thousand programs on display year-round—many at no cost—from local, national, and international artists, musicians, and dancers. Information about other Chicago attractions in the form of brochures, maps, and coupons, as well as live help and recommendations from representatives can be procured in the Chicago Visitor Information Center.

Tweens and Teens Tip: If you're feeling artsy when you leave, shop for souvenirs at one of two shops on the premises. Alternatively, deposit $5 into the Art-O-Mat machine (a retired cigarette vending machine), pull the knob, and go home with a real piece of art!

Chicago Riverwalk

On the south bank of the Chicago River, along Wacker Drive
Chicago
www.explorechicago.org
✪
Hours: Daily 6:00 a.m.–11:00 p.m.

Architect Daniel Burnham's "Master Plan of Chicago" was designed to flow with the Chicago River, and public access via a vibrant riverwalk was always an eventuality. After years of growth, the river-level promenade is now a true destination for visitors. Thanks to recent expansion efforts, the river is accessible from Franklin Street all the way to the lakefront.

In addition to the cafes and restaurants dotted along the way, visitors can pay respects to those who served our country at the Vietnam Veteran's Memorial at Wabash Plaza, learn about the history and behind-the-scenes workings of Chicago's bridges at the McCormick Tribune Bridgehouse and Chicago River Museum, and purchase tickets to tour the city by bike, boat or water taxi at various establishments.

Tweens and Teens Tip: Instead of cowering as you walk under the bridges, *look up*. The canopies installed to protect riverwalk pedestrians from trash that might fall from above are mirrored, giving a whole other dimension to the view of the water.

Chicago Trolley & Double Decker Company
Starting Point Varies
Chicago
(773) 648-5000
www.chicagotrolley.com
$$$$
Hours: Vary. Check the website for details.
Twitter: @chitrolley

The Chicago Trolley & Double Decker Company has entertained visitors since 1994, when the owners made a radical decision. Rather than hiring bus drivers and training them to give tours, they hired actors and comedians and taught them how to drive a trolley. That wise decision put the company on the map.

The most popular offering is the *Hop On Hop Off* tour that operates from 9 a.m. to 6 p.m. daily throughout the year except for Thanksgiving Day, Christmas Eve, and Christmas Day. The duration of the tour from start to finish is two hours; however, hopping off (and on!) the trolley (or bus) is encouraged so that your family can enjoy all the city has to offer.

Tweens and Teens Tip: You can catch a bus or trolley every fifteen minutes; if a full one arrives, just wait for the next one! One- and Multi-day passes are offered. See the website for a great map of the stops on the *Signature Tour* and the *North, West,* and *South Neighborhood Tours* in order to do a little advance planning. Check out "Touring Chicagoland" starting on page 189 for other companies that will show you the sights of the city.

Clarence Buckingham Memorial Fountain
Columbus Drive & Congress Parkway
Chicago
(312) 742-7648
www.chicagoparkdistrict.com
✪
Hours: Daily 8:00 a.m.–11:00 p.m.
Twitter: @chicagoparks

Dedicated in 1927 to the people of Chicago by Kate Buckingham in memory of her brother, the Buckingham Fountain is one of Chicago's most recognizable icons. An extremely popular destination for tourists and locals alike, it has been used as a backdrop in photos and films. The fountain, made of Georgia pink marble, originally cost $750,000 and has a water capacity of 1.5 million gallons. Edward H. Bennett designed the fountain itself to represent Lake Michigan; the four sea horses surrounding it stand for the four states that touch the lake: Wisconsin, Illinois, Indiana, and Michigan.

The fountain runs from 8:00 a.m. until 11:00 p.m. from April until mid-October, depending on the weather. Every hour on the hour, the center jet shoots water 150 feet in the air as part of a major water display that lasts for twenty minutes.

Tweens and Teens Tip: Visit the fountain on hot, summer nights: beginning at dusk (through 11:00 p.m.) there is an added light and music display which was created in part with help from Kate Buckingham herself. She worked with technicians when the various glass filters were tested to produce the essence of what you see today.

Museum

Federal Reserve Bank of Chicago Money Museum
230 S. LaSalle Street
Chicago
(312) 322-2400
www.chicagofed.org

✪

Hours: Mon–Fri (except on bank holidays) 8:30 a.m.–5:00 p.m.
Twitter: @chicagofed

If you've ever wanted to see — in person — what a million dollars looks like, then you're in the right place! The Federal Reserve Bank of Chicago Money Museum houses a cube full of one million one-dollar bills front and center for all to enjoy.

Visitors are first treated to a short video about exactly what it is that the Fed does, as well as a question and answer session. Visitors can then take a guided tour (Monday through Friday at 1:00 p.m.) of the exhibits themselves, but be forewarned: outsiders are not actually allowed anywhere near the vaults or the open money. The small museum can quench the thirst for knowledge about how our federal bank system works, but can't literally *show you the money*.

Tweens and Teens Tip: The website has an interactive tour if you want a preview of the exhibits.

The Field Museum

1400 S. Lake Shore Drive
Chicago
312-922-9410
www.fieldmuseum.org
$$$$
Hours: Daily 9:00 a.m.–5:00 p.m. (Closed on Christmas Day)
Twitter: @fieldmuseum

You don't have to be a natural history buff to have a great time exploring the Field; there's something here for nearly everyone. Collections on display include "Animals, Plants, & Ecosystems," "Rocks and Fossils," "The Ancient Americas," "Africa," "Asia and the Pacific," "The Americas," and more. Visitor favorite "Inside Ancient Egypt" features a walk-in tomb, more than twenty human mummies, and hieroglyphs that are 5,000 years old. Go to the north end of Stanley Field Hall to get a close-up look at Sue, the largest, most complete, and best-preserved T. rex fossil ever discovered.

Upstairs on the south end of the museum you'll find the recently renovated Grainger Hall of Gems. It is one of the best-loved areas of the museum and features rare jewels from every era, including some pieces from Tiffany & Co.

The museum offers free Highlights Tours to visitors; this is your chance to get the behind-the-scenes stories on some of the exhibits. Tours run at 11:00 a.m. and 2:00 p.m., Monday through Friday. When you need some downtime (and food), recharge at McDonald's and Corner Bakery, conveniently located inside the museum.

Tweens and Teens Tip: Check the website for a plethora of free admission days. Younger tweens, along with their parents, can spend the night in the museum with Sue the T. rex during "Dozin' with the Dinos," a twice-monthly night of family fun.

Food

Garrett Popcorn Shop
26 W. Randolph Street
Chicago
(888) 476-7267
www.garrettpopcorn.com
$
Hours: Mon–Sat 10:00 a.m.–8:00 p.m., Sun 11:00 a.m.–7:00 p.m.
Twitter: @garrettpopcorn

Also see Garrett Popcorn Shop, Chicago-North of the Loop.

Hostelling International-Chicago
24 East Congress Parkway
Chicago
312-360-0300
www.hichicago.org
$$$$$
Hours: 24/7
Twitter: @hostelchicago

HI-Chicago, otherwise known as The J. Ira and Nicki Harris Family Hostel, is an affordable alternative to downtown hotels for travelers and locals (outside of a zip code that begins with 606) alike. Because the hostel is located smack-dab in the middle of downtown Chicago, guests are within easy walking distance of Millennium and Grant Parks as well as the Museum Campus. Rooms sleep six or eight (in bunk beds), and a continental breakfast is included in the nightly rate. A self-service kitchen is accessible to all guests, and it's a great place within the hostel where you can spend time conversing with other travelers from all over the world.

The hostel offers daily volunteer-led events to all guests. If you would like to explore the city on your own, the knowledgeable staff can assist you with a plan and quite possibly find area discounts, as well. Other amenities include linens, towels, and pillows for all guests, and free WI-FI for those who need to stay connected.

Tweens and Teens Tip: Families of four can rent a room, which includes one full-sized bed and two singles. Local guests who have a home zip code that begins with 606 can only stay at the hostel if they are a part of a group of ten or more. Become a member of Hostelling International USA for a nominal fee to avoid a $3 per person, per night surcharge.

Hubbard Street Dance Chicago

Harris Theater for Music & Dance in Millennium Park
Chicago
(312) 850-9744
www.hubbardstreetdance.com
$$$–$$$$$
Hours: Vary. Check the website for performance details.
Twitter: @hubbardstreet

One of the top contemporary dance companies in the United States, Hubbard Street Dance Chicago, is as much known for its athleticism and agility as it is for its creative programming. Whether performing internationally or for a home audience at the Harris Theater for Music and Dance, the company's exciting and innovative repertoire entertains and inspires.

Constantly in a state of evolution, the small main company is one of the few to perform year-round. Hubbard Street 2 is a group of dancers between seventeen and twenty-five years old who perform in schools and community centers and is also a source for future members of the main company. Hubbard Street Dance sets out to motivate fans beyond the walls of the theater by performing community outreach with more than twenty local schools each year.

Tweens and Teens Tip: If you're on a budget, tickets for Hubbard Street 2 performances at the Harris Theater are extremely reasonable. If you want to get in on the act, sign up for dance classes offered by Hubbard Street Dance! Information is on the website.

Joffrey Ballet
50 E. Congress Parkway
Chicago
(312) 386-8905
www.joffrey.com
$$$$$
Hours: Performances are generally Wed/Fri/Sat 7:30 p.m. &
Sat/Sun 2:00 p.m. Check the website for details.
Twitter: @joffreyballet

Based in Chicago since 1995, the Joffrey Ballet was founded in New York in 1956 by Robert Joffrey and Gerald Arpino. Renowned for both classic and contemporary pieces, the company performs at the Auditorium Theater of Roosevelt University during its season, which lasts from October through May. Tickets can be purchased for individual performances or in a series.

Tchaikovsky's "The Nutcracker" is a Chicago tradition and is generally performed for three weeks in December. It features the entire Joffrey Company along with local children's choruses and over one hundred young dancers.

Tweens and Teens Tip: Student Rush tickets are available, while supplies last, for a deeply discounted price when you present a valid student I.D. at the box office within one hour of a performance.

Fun & Games

Kayak Chicago
Starting Points Vary
Chicago
630-336-7245
www.kayakchicago.com
$$$–$$$$$
Hours: 10:00 a.m.–7:00 p.m. on various days from Memorial Day–
September. Check the website for details.
Twitter: @kayakchicago

Kayaking, in Chicago? Absolutely! Water lovers of all levels can experience the city waterways from a kayak or paddleboard with a lesson, tour, or equipment rental. Warm weather starting point locations include the Chicago River at North Avenue, Montrose Beach, and Leone Beach. Off-season, classes are conducted at the UIC Indoor Pool.

Guided tours include: *Fireworks Paddle, Lake Paddle, Architectural/ History Paddle, Night Paddle,* and *Sunset Paddle.* If you'd rather skim the waters at your own pace, equipment can be rented for periods of an hour up to an entire day. The kayak rental fee includes everything you need: kayak, paddle, and life jacket. Waivers are required, but experience is not.

Tweens and Teens Tip: Kids (ages twelve and older) are allowed to paddle a single kayak; younger kids must paddle in a tandem with an adult. If you would like to use a tandem kayak, arrive early since reservations are not required.

Lakefront Trail

From Hollywood Avenue to 71st Street
Chicago
312-742-7529
www.chicagoparkdistrict.com/resources/beaches/
✪
Hours: 24/7

Enjoying Lake Michigan up close is made easy with 18 miles of paved trail that runs from Hollywood Avenue on the north end to 71st Street on the south end. The trail passes more than thirty beaches, numerous playgrounds, Lincoln Park Zoo, Navy Pier, Buckingham Fountain, Museum Campus, Soldier Field, McCormick Place, and more. It can be used for walking, jogging, skating, or biking. Maps are available online.

Tweens and Teens Tip: The Lakefront Trail is not only an easy path to use when traveling from Point A to Point B. If you have the time to slow down it's great for people watching, too.

Macy's on State Street

111 N. State Street
Chicago
(312) 781-4483
www.visitmacyschicago.com

♦

Hours: Mon–Sat 10:00 a.m.–8:00 p.m., Sun 11:00 a.m.–6:00 p.m.

This historical slice of Chicago once known as Marshall Field's on State (some locals will still not use the Macy's name when referring to this location) achieved National Historic Landmark status in 1979 and still contains most of what made it famous in the first place. A Mecca for clothing, cosmetics, house wares, and more, Macy's on State is a required pilgrimage for shopaholics everywhere, but that's not all. The seven-ton green clocks which hang outside and the Tiffany Favrile glass ceiling (containing over 1.6 million pieces) over the cosmetics department are only a few of the jewels contained in this local treasure.

If you get hungry while exploring, the seventh floor has a couple of options that will satisfy any palate. The Walnut Room, with its 17-foot fountain (and, at the holidays, its giant Christmas tree), is a Chicago tradition. If you are looking for something a little more casual, the Frango café serves sandwiches and great desserts featuring one of Chicago's favorite candies, the Frango Mint. Seven on State is an upscale food court with many offerings as well.

Tweens and Teens Tip: MP3 audio tours can be downloaded from the website in advance of a visit, so you can make the most of this quintessential Chicago shopping experience, whose sights, sounds, tastes—and even customer service—are unmatched.

Millennium Park

Bordered by Michigan Avenue, Columbus Drive,
Randolph Street, & Monroe Street
Chicago
312-742-1168
www.millenniumpark.org
✪
Hours: Daily 6:00 a.m.–11:00 p.m.
Twitter: @millennium_park

Though important enough to the city of Chicago that Daniel Burnham planned around it, the Illinois Central rail yard was an unsightly blob just north of the Grant Park area for more than half of the 20th century. Rumblings of beautifying the area began as early as 1977 and twenty years later, Mayor Richard M. Daley signed off on the first solid plans to develop on top of the still-in-use railroad tracks. What followed can only be described as the birth of the city's crown jewel: a massive, 24.5-acre park (officially opened in 2004) full of beautiful sights and sounds, and something for everybody.

Frank Gehry's Pritzker Pavilion is the beautiful setting for many music and dance performances. *Cloud Gate*, the sculpture created by artist Anish Kapoor (known to locals as "The Bean") is front and center, providing a reflection of the city from every direction. The Crown Fountain, with its morphing Chicago-resident faces that "spit" water on people of all ages throughout the summer, is a sight to see during the day as well as at night, when it is colorfully lit. Other must-see park features include the Lurie Garden, the BP Bridge, the Wrigley Square and Millennium Park Monument, the McCormick Tribune Plaza and Ice Rink, and the Boeing Galleries.

Tweens and Teens Tip: Before visiting, download the MP3 audio tour from the website to get detailed information about each feature in the park. Also, check out the newer Nichols Bridgeway, that connects Millennium Park to the third floor of the West Pavilion of the Art Institute.

Original Rainbow Cone

177 N. State Street (Inside the Halsted Street Deli)
Chicago
(312) 931-3354
www.rainbowcone.com
$$
Hours: Open seasonally from March to November; hours increase throughout the summer. Check website for details.
Twitter: @originalrainbow

Also see Original Rainbow Cone, Chicago-South of the Loop.

Segway Experience of Chicago

224 S. Michigan Avenue, Ste. 113
Chicago
(312) 663-0600
www.mysegwayexperience.com
$$$$$
Hours: Vary. Check the website for details.
Twitter: @segwayxchicago

Once the stuff of futuristic fantasies, the Segway Personal Transporter is becoming a fixture on college campuses, police beats, and now, Chicago tours. The green technology that operates these electric, two-wheeled vehicles uses many sensors along with dynamic stabilization. To put it simply, it's a little like walking. To move forward, lean forward a little bit. To move backward, lean back. Tilt the handlebar left or right when you want to make a turn.

The Segway Experience of Chicago is the only area Segway-authorized company using this modern method of transport. Tours offered include the *Park Glide Tour* (with photo stops in Millennium Park, Daley Bicentennial Plaza, the Lakefront Bike Path, Museum Campus, and Grant Park), the *Holiday Lights Tour*, and the *Chicago Architecture Foundation Tour*, as well as tours originating from Navy Pier (May through October only) that take participants to see various sights on the lakefront, in the parks, and through residential areas.

Tweens and Teens Tip: The minimum age to take a Segway for a glide is twelve. Participants who are twelve to fifteen years old can tour, but a parent must sign a waiver as well as participate. Those who are sixteen to seventeen years old do not need parental guidance but must present a signed waiver, and those eighteen and older require no parental permission.

Shedd Aquarium

1200 S. Lake Shore Drive
Chicago
312-939-2438
www.sheddaquarium.org
$$$$
Hours: Weekdays 9:00 a.m.–5:00 p.m., Weekends 9:00 a.m.–6:00 p.m.
Twitter: @shedd_aquarium

One of the three museum attractions at Museum Campus, the Shedd Aquarium has graced the shore of Lake Michigan for eighty years. Nearly two million people visit the Shedd each year, cementing its place at or near the top of any list of "must-see" Chicago attractions. The Shedd is home to more than 22,000 aquatic animals from around the world all of which help to educate the public about every aspect of marine life.

The Shedd's exhibits are divided by geographical location. The most popular exhibit and the centerpiece of the grand rotunda is the Caribbean Reef, which contains 90,000 gallons of water and is the home of moray eels, green sea turtles, sharks, and more. Visit the coast of the Pacific Northwest (and many favorite creatures) in the Oceanarium. Behind-the-scenes tours are offered periodically for an extra fee.

Tweens and Teens Tip: If possible, arrive early because the Shedd tends to get extremely busy by midday. A warning for those visiting during football season: there are parking restrictions at Museum Campus on Chicago Bears game days, so be sure to plan ahead. For families with deep pockets, the Shedd offers some unique experiences like Beluga Encounter and Trainer for a Day.

Skydeck Chicago

233 S. Wacker Drive
Chicago
312-875-9447
www.theskydeck.com
$$$$
Hours: Open 365 days a year. April–September 9:00 a.m.–10:00 p.m.,
October–March 10:00 a.m.–8:00 p.m.
Twitter: @skydeckchicago

Controversy boiled over in 2009 when Willis Group Holdings, Ltd (a London-based insurance broker) obtained the naming rights to the Sears Tower, which was the tallest building in the world when it was completed in 1974 and for almost 25 years after. Though the official name of the building is now the Willis Tower, most Chicago locals stand firm on referring to it by its former name. No matter the name, some of the best views of Chicago and beyond can be had from the 103rd floor.

The Skydeck experience includes a stop in the Skydeck Theater to see "Reaching for the Sky," an informative, nine-minute movie about advancements in Chicago architecture, as well as a faster-than-fast one-minute elevator ride up to the observation deck. Once there, visitors can find many things to look at in every direction. On a clear day, visibility is up to fifty miles and four states. An interactive exhibit detailing the history of the Sears/Willis Tower and Chicago is on the inner walls. If your party is adventurous, a step out onto the Ledge is in order. Four glass boxes extend 4.3 feet from the Skydeck, providing visitors with unobstructed—and, depending on the anxiety level, heart palpitating—views of the city below.

Tweens and Teens Tip: The lines for this attraction can literally stretch around the block. The best way to get to the top quickly is with a FastPass or CityPASS, which provides VIP access and express entry

45

to the elevators, as well as discounted admission to other city attractions. If the higher-priced ticket isn't in the budget, plan to arrive at opening time for the best shot at light crowds.

Chicago-North of the Loop

The area that is north of the Chicago River is more densely populated than any other area of the city. In addition to famous destinations that are close to the Loop like the Magnificent Mile, Lincoln Park Zoo, and Navy Pier, you will also find great neighborhoods to explore. Wrigleyville (home of the Chicago Cubs and a culture all its own), Old Town (theater, shopping, entertainment), Lincoln Square (German specialties, hip boutiques), Rogers Park (diverse immigrant population, college town), and Lakeview (vast options in dining, shopping, and entertainment) are just a few. Though the neighborhood boundaries seem blurry, each area has its own distinctive voice.

American Science & Surplus
5316 N. Milwaukee Avenue
Chicago
(773) 763-0313
www.sciplus.com
Hours: Mon–Wed 10:00 a.m.–7:00 p.m., Thurs 10:00 a.m.–8:00 p.m.,
Fri 10:00 a.m.–7:00 p.m., Sat 10:00 a.m.–6:00 p.m.,
Sun 11:00 a.m.–5:00 p.m.
Twitter: @sciplus

You don't have to be a geek to enjoy this collection of gadgets, parts, crafts, books, and whatchamacallits all under one roof. Like Uncle Fun (see page 77), American Science & Surplus is a veritable Disney World to a kid with only a couple of bucks in his pocket. Founded around 1937 as "American Lens & Photo," AS & S soon expanded its inventory with war surplus items, and over the years gradually became home to (and focused on) science and educational products.

Strolling through the aisles can take some time if you don't want to miss anything. This is not a "run in and get what you want, then leave" kind of store. The wise family sets aside at least an hour to let the kiddies pick out their test tubes, crime scene tape, lava lamps, motors, magnets, prisms, Russian military paraphernalia, craft supplies, and anything else that happens to come off the truck that week. New items arrive all the time, so each visit is a different kind of fun.

Tweens and Teens Tip: Though they can't possibly know *every* tidbit of information about every single item in the store, the shelf tags are written by the ever-knowledgeable staff in a manner that will not only clue you in on what you're seeing, but also keep you laughing throughout the duration of your visit.

Blue Man Group

3133 N. Halsted Street
Chicago
(773) 348-4000
www.blueman.com
$$$$$
Hours: Performances Tuesday through Sunday.
Check the website for details.
Twitter: @bluemangroup

Feeling Blue? Never fear, Blue Man Group is here! Briar Street Theatre has been the home of this azure-colored trio since 1997, and their popularity ensures that they're not leaving anytime soon. The show is difficult to describe, and the act of even trying to explain it is certainly discouraged as the experience is best enjoyed without any preconceived notions of what it's about. What most people have learned about the Blue Men from commercials is enough: they are blue, they have a quirky sense of humor, and they are amazing percussionists. Enough said.

The show is one hour, forty-five minutes long with no intermission. Tickets are released for sale approximately eight weeks in advance. It should be noted that the first seven rows are in the "Poncho Section" (ponchos are provided), and the balcony seats are partially obstructed. Strobe lights are used during the performance, and the theatre recommends that children younger than five do not attend. The Group Sales department is always very helpful in making arrangements for large get-togethers. A couple of audience members are chosen in each performance to assist the Blue Men, and that random ingredient makes the show even more unpredictable and usually rolling-on-the-floor funny.

Tweens and Teens Tip: The lobby is full of little surprises! While waiting for the House to open, pass the time by discovering them.

A coat check and beverages are available. Don't forget to visit the restrooms either, because the piped-in music hints at the flavor of the show you're about to see. A limited amount of Student Rush tickets can be purchased at a reduced rate (with a high school or college identification card) at the Box Office within two hours of the show.

The Boring Store
1331 N. Milwaukee Avenue
Chicago
(773) 772-8108
www.826chi.org

♦

Hours: 12:00 p.m.–6:00 p.m. Daily
Twitter: @theboringstore

If your family includes a young secret agent, you're in luck: The Boring Store is the place to stock up on needed spy gear for any undercover assignment. Supplies are packaged in the most boring way possible (brown paper wrappers with a nondescript label), so that nobody's cover is blown upon purchase.

Items for sale include decoding pens, standard "eavesdroppers" (which are really just average drinking glasses), tote bags, spy notebooks, and more. Books written by groups of local students are also available in the store.

Tweens and Teens Tip: Purchases at The Boring Store have deeper impact: proceeds go directly to 826CHI, the creative writing and tutoring lab for local students.

Chicago Pizza and Oven Grinder Company

2121 N. Clark Street
Chicago
(773) 248-2570
www.chicagopizzaandovengrinder.com
$$
Hours: Mon–Thurs 4:00 p.m.–11:00 p.m., Fri 4:00 p.m.–12:00 a.m.,
Sat 12:00 p.m.–12:00 a.m., Sun 12:00 p.m.–11:00 p.m.

While Chicago is known for deep-dish pizza, and while it is actually home to great establishments that specialize in the other types of pizza like Neapolitan and Margherita, there is one restaurant which is truly one of a kind on any "Best of" list, and that is Chicago Pizza and Oven Grinder Company. Their twist is actually a pizza pot pie. Available in half pound or one pound sizes and with white or wheat dough, this gooey, cheesy, meaty creation is something you won't find anywhere else. The other house special is the oven grinder, which is a baked Italian loaf stuffed with Italian meats, cheese, and peppers. The menu also includes salads and flatbreads.

First-time visitors are confused by the fact that, even with waits of one to two hours, the host does not take names because *he remembers faces*. This element adds to the mysterious and kitschy feel of the place, whose history is just as interesting as the menu. The St. Valentine's Day Massacre of February 14, 1929 occurred in a garage across the street and it is rumored that the Chicago Pizza and Oven Grinder Company house was used as a lookout. Decades later in November 1971, the place was gutted by fire and has since, of course, been restored and renovated to something as close to its original glory as possible.

Tweens and Teens Tip: Credit cards are no good at Chicago Pizza and Oven Grinder Company; you must pay cash. Because reservations are not accepted, choose your dinnertime wisely if you don't want to wait during peak hours.

Chicago Shakespeare Theater

800 East Grand Avenue
Chicago
312-595-5600
www.chicagoshakes.com
$$$$$
Hours: Performances daily, with the exception of Monday.
Twitter: @chicagoshakes

While some might shy away at the very mention of Shakespeare, this theater has a great reputation for making the Bard seem like a friend instead of a foe. The company's six hundred shows in each year's 48-week season are performed in a beautiful facility smack dab in the middle of Navy Pier. The Courtyard Theater, which is the primary venue for performances, seats 510 spectators in the round. The theater has three seating levels and a thrust stage that extends into the audience's area: there is really not a bad seat in the house. The Upstairs Theater is much smaller and unadorned with seating for 200.

The company performs several Shakespearian masterpieces each season along with modern classic pieces, occasionally featuring the Chicago Chamber Musicians. Pre- and post-performance talks about the historical context of the plays (and how they are relevant in today's society) are offered to audiences, which help to make the CST experience not only enjoyable but also educational.

Tweens and Teens Tip: At least once per season, CST performs a "Short Shakespeare" piece, which is geared towards younger and new-to-Shakespeare audiences. The shows are 75-minutes long and include a post-show question session with the actors. Don't forget to have your Navy Pier parking garage ticket validated in the lobby to save 40%!

Show

ComedySportz Chicago

929 W. Belmont Avenue
Chicago
(773) 549-8080
www.comedysportzchicago.com
$$$$
Hours: Performances are Thurs 8:00 p.m., Fri 8:00 p.m. &
10:00 p.m., Sat 6:00 p.m., 8:00 p.m., 10:00 p.m.
Twitter: @comedysportzchi

Improvisational comedy didn't become popular overnight. Casts of television shows like "Saturday Night Live," "MADtv," and "Whose Line Is It Anyway?" have been recruited from local theaters for years. The speed, hilarity, and often brilliance of improv comedy makes it a shoo-in for families with older children, especially if you can find an improv troupe that uses clean humor. ComedySportz is one of those troupes.

The short-form improv performed at ComedySportz is actually a competition between two teams, the red and the blue. The audience votes and chooses a winner prior to intermission. In the second half, the teams return and use audience volunteers on stage as a part of the show.

Tweens and Teens Tip: Due to the spontaneity and variety of improv games, every show is different. Though the shows at ComedySportz Chicago are family-friendly, the crowds vary according to show time. Expect lots more younger children at the earlier shows, and a rowdier audience made up of mostly adults at the later shows.

Ed Debevic's

640 N. Wells Street
Chicago
(312) 664-1707
www.eddebevics.com
$$$
Hours: Mon–Thurs 11:00 a.m.–9:00 p.m., Fri 11:00 a.m.–11:00 p.m.,
Sat 9:00 a.m.–11:00 p.m., Sun 9:00 a.m.–9:00 p.m.

"Eat and Get Out!" is the motto of this 50s style, raucously-staffed diner that is for the family who doesn't mind a little noise (and possibly a few insults) with their meal. All employees invent their alter-ego upon hire and are in character, complete with costume and an alias, like Cookie or Squeakers. Upon approaching the hostess' station, you may or may not be greeted by an employee. (Customers who are unaware of the Ed's environment might be put off by the rudeness at first but generally catch on quickly.) As the hostess eventually leads you to your table, she will likely yell at another employee — or customer — to "Mooooove!"

Servers tell it like it is and educate their guests on the pecking order immediately. You may overhear servers say things like, "Here's how it works. I'm gonna be rude to you, and you're gonna like it." Though the loud and seemingly unbridled atmosphere might imply that service is lacking, in truth the staff really know what they're doing and guests who are open-minded about the experience will have a great time. And the food's not bad, either! While you enjoy traditional diner-fare like grilled cheese, burgers, and Ed's Mom's Meatloaf, the staff entertains with dancing and contests. Finish the experience off with the World's Smallest Ice Cream Sundae, served in a shot glass, and then . . . get out!

Tweens and Teens Tip: Tweens and teens love this place, of course; seeing their parents spoken to in a manner that they only wish they could get away with makes for a fun evening. Souvenirs (t-shirts and such) can be purchased on the way out . . . if you can find someone who is willing to be of assistance!

Tour

Eli's Cheesecake Factory Tour
6701 W. Forest Preserve Drive
Chicago
(773) 736-3417
www.elicheesecake.com
$
Hours: Tours are conducted Mon–Fri at 1:00 p.m. for walk-ins
(other times available by reservation).
Store hours: Mon–Fri 8:00 a.m.–6:00 p.m., Sat 9:00 a.m.–5:00 p.m.,
Sun 11:00 a.m.–5:00 p.m.
Twitter: @elischeesecake

One of the most famous foods out of Chicago, Eli's cheesecake is like no other. In fact, it has played an important role in historical events like President Bill Clinton's inauguration and Chicago's 150th birthday, and it is a mainstay at the annual Taste of Chicago Festival in Grant Park.

What many local folks don't know is that the Eli's Cheesecake Factory is open to the public for tours. Several different tour options are available; the basic tour only costs a couple of dollars. It includes a short video on the history of the company and a walk through the test kitchen as well as the cheesecake kitchen (the sight of the massive cooling racks is impressive in itself!). Best of all, each participant receives a slice of cheesecake at the end.

Tweens and Teens Tip: Before leaving the facility, shop for "seconds," cheesecakes (flavors vary each day!) that are flawed in appearance but have the same outstanding taste and sold at heavily discounted prices!

Garrett Popcorn Shop

625 N. Michigan Avenue (Flagship Store)
Chicago
(888) 476-7267
www.garrettpopcorn.com
$
Hours: Mon–Thurs 10:00 a.m.–8:00 p.m.,
Fri–Sat 10:00 a.m.–10:00 p.m., Sun 10:00 a.m.–7:00 p.m.
Twitter: @garrettpopcorn

A Chicago tradition since 1949, Garrett Popcorn Shops (referred to as "Garrett's" by most locals) are so popular that locals know it's worth it to stand in the out-the-door lines to purchase a bag or two of their delicious product. Though the popcorn is available in many varieties including Buttery, Macadamia CaramelCrisp, Almond Caramel-Crisp, Cashew CaramelCrisp, and Pecan CaramelCrisp, it's the regular CaramelCrisp, the CheeseCorn, and the mix of both—called the Chicago Mix—that has fans over the moon.

In addition to the flagship store on Michigan Avenue, Garrett's has five other locations in the downtown area: 600 East Grand Avenue (Navy Pier), 26 West Randolph Street (next to the Oriental Theatre), 4 East Madison Street (State Street & Madison), 2 West Jackson Boulevard (State Street & Jackson), and 222 Merchandise Mart Plaza (Merchandise Mart, second level Food Court). The Ogilvie Transportation Center is home to one shop, and O'Hare Airport has two of them, inside terminals one and three (past the security checkpoints).

Tweens and Teens Tip: If you yearn for a taste of Garrett's after returning home, tins full of the sweet and salty treat are available for purchase via the online store: they'll ship anywhere in the United States and to limited international destinations (extra fees may apply).

Green City Market

1750 N. Clark Street (Outdoor)
2430 N. Cannon Drive (Indoor)
Chicago
(773) 880-1266
www.greencitymarket.org

♦

Hours: Sat 8:00 a.m.–1:00 p.m. (November–April),
Wed & Sat 7:00 a.m.–1:00 p.m. (May–October)
Twitter: @greencitymarket

Public enthusiasm for supporting sustainable farmer's markets has increased in record numbers over the past decade. Concern with where food comes from is on the rise, as is the desire to be healthier by eating simple foods from the earth. The Green City Market, founded in 1998, is Chicago's only year-round, sustainable farmer's market.

Green City Market's mission statement (from their website), "to improve the availability of a diverse range of high quality foods, to connect local producers and farmers to chefs, restaurateurs, food organizations and the public, and to support small family farms and promote a healthier society through education and appreciation for local, fresh, sustainably raised produce and products" is achieved daily through their extensive events calendar, which includes cooking demonstrations, lectures, and workshops. Rick Bayless (Frontera Grill, Topolobampo, Xoco), Stephanie Izard (Girl and the Goat), and Ina Pinkney (Ina's) are only three of the many local chefs who support the Green City Market by shopping at the Market and/or participating in Market events.

During the colder months, the indoor market is located at the Peggy Notebaert Nature Museum (2430 N. Cannon Drive, Lincoln Park). During the warm months, the outdoor market is located on the south end of Lincoln Park between Clark Street and Stockton Drive.

Tweens and Teens Tip: Emerging foodies will enjoy the cooking demonstrations (offered twice weekly) presented by chefs who are at the top of their field. Demonstrations are free and first come/first served. Reservations are not required. Subscribe to the Green City Market's weekly e-newsletter to stay apprised of chef demonstration dates as well as detailed information about all Market programming.

Museum

International Museum of Surgical Science
1524 N. Lake Shore Drive
Chicago
(312) 642-6502
www.imss.org
$$
Hours: Tues-Sun 10:00 a.m.–4:00 p.m. (May–September),
Tues–Sat 10:00 a.m.–4:00 p.m. (October–April)

For something a little bit off the beaten path, spend some time in the four-story mansion housing this very unique museum which celebrates how medical procedures and technology have changed (and improved) through the ages. The largest part of the collections is made of medical artifacts and instruments, and visitors can also peruse artwork and sculptures that portray individuals or procedures. The Hall of Murals includes twelve oil paintings that illustrate surgical progress throughout history.

Parking is limited supply at IMSS, so public transportation is a good option for visitors. Be sure to check out the gift shop during your visit for all kinds of interesting souvenirs!

Tweens and Teens Tip: IMSS is a very small museum, and families who live outside of the city should plan an additional area activity in addition to make the trip downtown worthwhile. A student discount is available, so be sure to bring a school I.D.

John Hancock Observatory

875 N. Michigan Avenue, 94th Floor
Chicago
(888) 875-VIEW
www.hancockobservatory.com
$$$$
Hours: Sun–Sat 9:00 a.m.–11:00 p.m.
Twitter: @athousandfeetup

One of the top two iconic skyscrapers in Chicago, the John Hancock building, is fantastically beautiful on the exterior, but the views you can enjoy from inside are even more so. Check out the bird's eye, 360-degree view of Chicago and the states of Illinois, Indiana, Michigan and Wisconsin. Knowing what you're looking enhances the experience, so be sure to pick up a free Multimedia Sky Tour gadget. Chicago's Lookingglass Theatre Company co-founder (and star of the sitcom "Friends") David Schwimmer becomes your tour guide as he narrates stories about local history and important places.

The open-air Skywalk is a safe way to be outdoors on the 94th floor, and it's equipped with telescopes that have informational audio recordings and sound effects of the ground level attractions. Be sure to check out the eighty feet of murals that depict the history of Chicago.

Tweens and Teens Tip: For just a few dollars more than the cost of general admission, you can purchase a "Sun & Stars" pass. This pass gives you entry privileges in the morning and again at night. If you need some suggestions on how to best use your day in between visits, the John Hancock Observatory offers complimentary concierge service between 10:00 a.m. and 7:00 p.m.

Zoo

Lincoln Park Zoo
2001 N. Clark Street
Chicago
(312) 742-2000
www.lpzoo.org
✪
Hours: Weekdays 10:00 a.m.–5:00 p.m.,
Weekends 10:00 a.m.–6:30 p.m. (Memorial Day–Labor Day only: the
zoo closes earlier during the winter. Check website before you go!)
Twitter: @lincolnparkzoo

Open 365 days a year, the Lincoln Park Zoo is fun for all ages. With the exception of the $19 parking fee for visitors who drive there, zoo admission is still free, which means that a day at the zoo is a great value for families. In addition to the animal exhibits, which include such favorites as the Kovler Sea Lion Pool and the Regenstein Center for African Apes, the family can also take advantage of special programs like "Exploring Ape Behavior." In this hands-on program, participants observe one of the zoo's gorillas or chimpanzees and record what they see on an iPod Touch. (Contact the zoo for registration.)

Tweens and Teens Tip: If the zoo is a family favorite, consider becoming a member. Free parking is offered to members, as are discounts on events, food, retail, and educational opportunities.

Museum of Contemporary Art

220 E. Chicago Avenue
Chicago
(312) 280-2660
www.mcachicago.org
$$
Hours: Tues 10:00 a.m.–8:00 p.m., Wed–Sun 10:00 a.m.–5:00 p.m.
Twitter: @mcachicago

Paintings, sculptures, photos, videos, and performance art pieces created since 1945 make up the collection of the Museum of Contemporary Art, located just one block east of Michigan Avenue in the Streeterville area. Of the more than 2,500 objects in the collection, a small amount is on display at any given time (along with temporary traveling exhibits). Every work of art has a wall label so that visitors can learn about it and the artist who created it.

Puck's at the MCA is the full-service restaurant (and express counter) conceptualized by the museum and chef Wolfgang Puck. A meal here will extend the modern art experience, and museum admission is not required of restaurant patrons.

Tweens and Teens Tip: Free 45-minute tours of the MCA are given by docents for those who want to delve deeper into the artwork on display.

Music Box Theatre

3733 N. Southport Avenue
Chicago
(773) 871-6604
www.musicboxtheatre.com
$$
Hours: Vary. Check website for details.
Twitter: @musicboxtheatre

The Music Box Theatre has a rich history. When it originally opened way back in 1929, it was considered to be a more "intimate" theater than most since it had seating for only 800. Unlike the larger movie palaces of the day, the Music Box had no stage for live productions. Equipped to show motion pictures with sound, it also housed an orchestra pit and organ chambers. In the event that the sound pictures failed, a silent movie could still be accompanied by music. The architectural elements suggest a combination of several different styles, however, the true and only style of the theatre is considered "atmospheric." The sky-like ceiling, dark with twinkling "stars," in combination with the heavily ornamented plaster walls accented with tall columns, makes a cozy, garden-like surrounding for guests.

All kinds of films have been shown here. These days, the theatre screens approximately 300 independent, cult, and foreign films per year. From classic film matinees to midnight show times, there's something here for everybody.

Tweens and Teens Tip: Visit the website to print out a movie schedule that covers a couple of months at a time. Want to save on admission? The theatre offers a five-admission ticket at a pretty good savings. Use the multiple admission ticket to pay for up to two people per visit.

Navy Pier

600 East Grand Avenue
Chicago
312-595-PIER
www.navypier.com
◆

Hours: Mon–Thurs 10:00 a.m.–8:00 p.m., Fri–Sat
10:00 a.m.–10:00 p.m., Sun 10:00 a.m.–7:00 p.m. (Winter hours);
Sun–Thurs 10:00 a.m.–10:00 p.m., Fri–Sat
10:00 a.m.–12:00 midnight (Summer hours).
Hours vary in spring and fall; check the website for details.
Twitter: @navypier

The number one tourist attraction in the Midwest has a colorful history. The only one of five piers included in Daniel Burnham's "Master Plan of Chicago" that was actually completed, Navy Pier opened in 1916 as Municipal Pier, a place for recreational activities along with freight and passenger ship docking facilities. During World War I, the pier was used to house soldiers, the Red Cross, and Home Defense units. Later it was renamed Navy Pier to salute the Navy personnel who served during World War I. Navy Pier was used for pilot training orientation during World War II and eventually became the home of a University of Illinois branch campus. By the 1970's, Navy Pier was no longer being used. It took more than twenty years for the state to create the Metropolitan Pier and Exposition authority (MPEA), whose purpose was to redesign Navy Pier and transform it into what it is today.

The transformation has been going on since 1995, and visitors have been flocking to Navy Pier ever since. It's home to rides and attractions like the iconic Ferris wheel, an 18-hole miniature golf course, and a musical carousel. Amazing Chicago's Funhouse is also at the Pier, along with hubs for Bike and Roll Chicago and the Segway Experience of Chicago. The Smith Museum of Stained Glass Windows, the

Chicago Children's Museum, and the Chicago Shakespeare Theater are here, as are dozens of kiosks, gift shops, and food outlets (everything from fast-food to fine dining).

Tweens and Teens Tip: Perhaps one of the best bargains in the entire downtown area, the Navy Pier parking garage costs only $20 per day (the full 24 hours) during the week and $24 on the weekends. Park and enjoy Navy Pier or take other modes of transport (free trolleys, water taxis, Segways, bicycles, or just walk!) from there to other downtown areas.

Noble Horse Theatre

1410 N. Orleans Street
Chicago
(312) 266-7878
www.noblehorsechicago.com
$$$$
Hours: Shows are performed at various times,
Wednesdays through Saturdays.

The Old Town area of Chicago is the setting for the Noble Horse Theatre, the only remaining riding hall and urban indoor horse performance theatre in North America. Three 60-75 minute shows are performed in the climate-controlled theatre during the year: "Quadrille: The Mystique of the Horse," "The Legend of Sleepy Hollow," and "The Nutcracker on Horseback."

Tiered seating ensures that every spot in the audience has great visibility. Dinner is optional for the evening shows, but spectators are welcome to bring their own snacks and drinks. After each show, free carriage rides are offered to the audience.

Tweens and Teens Tip: Stable tours are available before or after the show upon request. Bring apples or carrots if you'd like to give the horses a snack after the show!

Fun & Games

North Avenue Beach

1603 N. Lake Shore Drive
Chicago
312-742-PLAY
www.chicagoparkdistrict.com

✪

Hours: Daily 9:00 a.m.–9:30 p.m. (Memorial Day–Labor Day only)

If you ask someone about beaches in Chicago, the odds are pretty good that North Avenue Beach would be mentioned very quickly. The Lincoln Park area playground is teeming with swimming, tanning, jogging, rollerblading, volleyball-playing crowds all summer long. It is also the home of a distinctive Chicago landmark, the North Avenue Beach House.

The current North Avenue Beach House, built in the late 1990s to replace the original, outdated Depression-era house, is ocean-liner inspired and indeed better serves the plethora of beach visitors with concession stands, a lifeguard station, outdoor showers, restrooms, and rental offices for bikes, chairs, and volleyball equipment.

Tweens and Teens Tip: Look beyond the North Avenue Beach House to find the Chess Pavilion. Here you can play the classic game of strategy and logic on concrete game boards (or bring your own) while enjoying a breezy summer day at the beach.

North Park Village Nature Center

5801 N. Pulaski Road
Chicago
312-744-5472
www.chicagoparkdistrict.com
✪
Hours: 10:00 a.m.–4:00 p.m. Daily

City dwellers love this forty-six acre oasis in the middle of the hustle and bustle. A visit to the nature preserve is a great opportunity to enjoy flora and fauna up close. The area includes walking trails through savannas, wetlands, prairies and woodlands. Deer sightings are common here and, of course, there are birds, turtles, and other animals to be found.

Leave Fido at home when visiting the Nature Center, because dogs aren't allowed. Jogging, biking and fishing are also prohibited. Explore on foot to make the most of your inner-city nature experience. Parking is plentiful and free.

Tweens and Teens Tip: Special events at the North Park Village Nature Center include Concerts in the Parks, the Maple Syrup Festival, the Owl Prowl, free bird watching tours, and much more. Check the website for dates and times.

Tour

O'Leary's Chicago Fire Truck Tours

505 N. Michigan Avenue
Chicago
(312) 287-6565
www.olearysfiretours.com
$$$
Hours: Vary. Check website for details.

History fans fascinated with the implications of the Great Chicago Fire of 1871 will enjoy this unique view of the city. Tours are led by retired Chicago Fire Department Captain George Rabiela, a man whose desire to educate others has become a second career. Passengers ride in style, as Captain G drives a 26-passenger Mack Truck or, for bigger groups, a 36-passenger Pirsch Convertible Cab.

Stops include Chicago fire stations and the Chicago Fire Academy among others. Tours leave from the corner of Michigan and Illinois Streets. Reservations are required.

Tweens and Teens Tip: Many theories abound as to how the Great Chicago Fire actually began. The most well known is the story of Catherine O'Leary's cow kicking over a lantern in the barn behind 137 Dekoven Street. No matter what really happened, there is no denying that the fire, which destroyed about five square miles, was responsible for the creation of one of the world's great cities. Learning about it from a real-life Fire Department Captain is a great opportunity!

Peggy Notebaert Nature Museum
2430 N. Cannon Drive
Chicago
(773) 755-5100
www.chias.org
$$
Hours: Mon–Fri 9:00 a.m.–5:00 p.m., Sat–Sun 10:00 a.m.–5:00 p.m.
Twitter: @naturemuseum

For more than 150 years, the Chicago Academy of Sciences has made natural history specimens available to the public. Early on, the collections were destroyed by the Great Chicago Fire in 1871 but were later rebuilt and accompanied by dioramas, photography, lectures, and publications. In 1999, the Peggy Notebaert Nature Museum opened, giving the Academy a new home for its extensive collection as well as an interactive experience for visitors.

Permanent exhibitions like the "Judy Istock Butterfly Haven," "Mysteries of the Marsh," and the "Wilderness Walk" provide entertainingly educational moments and food for thought for young nature lovers.

Tweens and Teens Tip: Don't miss the First Flight Butterfly Release, daily at 2 p.m.! Also, check out the work of Chicago artist Amy Lowry on display in the conference room (admission is by request only).

The Signature Room at the 95th

875 N. Michigan Avenue
Chicago
(312) 787-9596
www.signatureroom.com
$$$$$
Hours: Sun 10:00 a.m.–2:00 p.m. (Brunch) & 5:00 p.m.–10:00 p.m.
(Dinner), Mon-Thurs 11:00 a.m.–2:30 p.m. (Lunch) &
5:00 p.m.–10:00 p.m. (Dinner), Fri-Sat 11:00 a.m.–2:30 p.m.
(Lunch) & 5:00 p.m.–11:00 p.m. (Dinner)
Twitter: @signatureroom95

Celebrating a special occasion takes on a whole new dimension when you enter one of Chicago's most celebrated buildings — the John Hancock — and soar up to the 95th floor in an express elevator. As the elevator doors open, the city unfolds itself right before your very eyes. Whether your party indulges in lunch, dinner, or Sunday brunch "in the sky," the staff of this elegant, art deco-style restaurant is completely committed to caring for every detail.

Chicago natives and visitors alike are awestruck at this unique view of the Windy City, which, combined with uncompromisingly superior service, makes a meal here completely unforgettable. An added bonus: with advance notice, the pastry chef will personalize a dessert for the guest of honor.

Tweens and Teens Tip: Though the nighttime city view is breathtaking, the daytime view is just as impressive. Save big bucks by enjoying the extensive lunch menu. If you aren't interested in a full meal and just want a snack with your skyline, head up to the Signature Lounge on the 96th Floor. Minors are allowed (accompanied by parents) and the menu includes appetizers and desserts to satisfy your hunger.

Smith Museum of Stained Glass Windows

Navy Pier
Chicago
312-595-5063
www.navypier.com

✪

Hours: Sun–Thurs 10:00 a.m.–8:00 p.m.,
Fri–Sat 10:00 a.m.–10:00 p.m.
Twitter: @navypier

Featuring 150 stained glass windows representing the years from 1870 to present-day, the Smith Museum of Stained Glass Windows is the first museum in the United States dedicated solely to stained glass windows. This hidden gem is tucked away inside Navy Pier and is free to the public. The windows are on display in a series of galleries in the 800-foot-long space. Both secular and religious windows are on display.

The windows are divided into four categories: Victorian, Prairie, Modern, and Contemporary. Of special note, the Richard H. Dreihaus Gallery of Stained Glass contains a collection of thirteen windows by none other than Louis Comfort Tiffany himself, along with his workshop. The Smith Museum is a quiet respite from the glaring, noisy environs of the rest of Navy Pier and families can benefit from a stroll through its peaceful corridors.

Tweens and Teens Tip: Enjoy the windows on a higher level by joining Museum Curator Rolf Achilles for a free public tour of the museum, on *most* Thursdays at 2:00 p.m.

Superdawg

6363 N. Milwaukee Avenue
Chicago
(773) 763-0660
www.superdawg.com
$$
Hours: Sun–Thurs 11:00 a.m.–1:00 a.m.,
Fri–Sat 11:00 a.m.–2:00 a.m.
Twitter: @superdawg

Maurie and Flaurie Berman, Superdawg founders, probably had no idea that their little drive-in hot dog stand on the corner of Milwaukee at Devon and Nagle would become a Chicago staple for more than sixty years (and counting!). The stand, visible from afar because of the two giant hot dog statues on the roof (not-so-coincidentally also named Maurie and Flaurie) is a hit with people of all ages. Its popularity, kitsch, and—not least of all—food, have caused this "little eatery that could" to be featured on countless television programs and in magazines galore. It is even included in Patricia Schultz's best-selling book 1,000 Places to See Before You Die: A Traveler's Life List.

What has made Superdawg so successful? The answers are numerous. The obvious? The all-beef Superdawgs, which are presented in the same manner they were back in the day: on poppy seed buns and topped with the standard ingredients (mustard, piccalilli, a kosher dill pickle, chopped Spanish onions, and a hot pepper), nestled in retro-style boxes among piles of delicious Superfries. (In fact, many of the menu items are named "Super-this" and "Whooper-that," which just scream out "Fun to eat!")

Tweens and Teens Tip: It gets harder and harder these days to find a real drive-in dining experience. Maurie and Flaurie have preserved this American tradition beautifully, and the entire family will love having their food delivered to them by carhops.

Swedish American Museum

5211 N. Clark Street
Chicago
(773) 728-8111
www.swedishamericanmuseum.org
$
Hours: Mon–Fri 10:00 a.m.–4:00 p.m., Sat–Sun 11:00 a.m.–4:00 p.m.
Twitter: @SwedeAmerican

It seems fitting that the Swedish American Museum is located in the Andersonville neighborhood, because Swedish immigrant residents were originally the overwhelming majority. One of them, Kurt Mathiasson, opened the original museum location in a log cabin in 1976. His mission was to preserve the Swedish-American heritage in Chicago. Family histories were collected and stored there.

In 1987 the museum moved to its 24,000 square-foot Clark Street location and is the major feature in a center that includes the Brunk Children's Museum of Immigration (suggested for children ages 3–12), a library, a genealogy center, and museum store. A special exhibit gallery houses four temporary exhibits annually. The permanent exhibit, "A Dream of America: Swedish Immigration to Chicago," is located on the second floor and follows Swedish immigrants on the journey from their homeland. The Museum hosts four major events every year including Midsommarfest (in June), which celebrates the summer solstice.

Tweens and Teens Tip: The Nordic Family Genealogy Center offers monthly classes and might inspire you to dig into areas of family history that are unfamiliar. Sessions are free to museum members and $10 per session for non-members. A schedule of other programs and special events is published twice annually.

Tall Ship Windy

700 E. Grand Avenue

Chicago

312-451-2700

www.tallshipadventuresofchicago.com

$$$$

Hours: Many sails are offered daily from Memorial Day through
September 30 only; check website for details.

Explore the city skyline from the Windy, Chicago's Official Tall Ship since 2006, when Mayor Richard M. Daley awarded it that distinction. The Windy is a 148-foot, four-masted gaff topsail schooner built in the traditional style with modern materials, features (like pressurized plumbing) and safety items. It can accommodate up to 150 passengers and is operated by Lakeshore Sail Charters.

The crew of the Windy offers many different sailing experiences, from relaxing sightseeing trips to hands-on, working sails. Depending on which adventure you choose, you can learn about environmental science, the life of a tall ship sailor, Chicago maritime history, Rum Runners of the 1930's, city architecture, and much more. The variety of offerings ensures that a family can make many return trips for a different experience each time. Sailing adventures are generally 90 minutes to two hours long, and all ages are welcome.

Tweens and Teens Tip: Lakeshore Sail Charters offers extensive educational programming for scout troops, schools, and youth groups. Enjoy a fireworks cruise that will create magical memories on Wednesday and Saturday evenings each summer.

Uncle Fun

1338 W. Belmont Avenue
Chicago
(773) 477-8223
www.unclefunchicago.com
Hours: Mon–Fri 12:00 p.m.–7:00 p.m., Sat 11:00 a.m.–7:00 p.m.,
Sun 11:00 a.m.–5:00 p.m.
Twitter: @unclefunchicago

The name says it all. Kids of all ages are blown away by the offerings of this Good Times Headquarters on the North side. The store is chock-full of whoopee cushions, postcards, magic tricks, vintage toys, bobble heads, harmonicas, and thousands of other items that change all the time and come from all over the world.

With a knowledgeable staff always more than ready to demonstrate how trick gum works or ask customers probing questions to help find that unique item to take home, visits to Uncle Fun are never boring and never the same.

Tweens and Teens Tip: Check out the website to taste the flavor of Uncle Fun before your visit. Also, because prices range from mere pennies on up to amounts for which paper money is needed, tweens and teens on any budget will be able to have fun while staying within their means.

Wrigley Field Tours

1060 W. Addison Street
Chicago
(773) 404-CUBS
http://chicago.cubs.mlb.com/chc/ballpark/tours/index.jsp
$$$$
Hours: Tours are given April-October. Check website for details.
Twitter: @wrigley_field

A must for any die-hard fan of the Chicago Cubs (though not limited to them!), tours of Wrigley Field provide a new perspective beyond the game itself. Stops on the tour can include the press box, the dugout, clubhouses, on-deck circles, box suites, the visitor's locker room, and more. Depending on the weather or what's going on at the field that day, certain areas may be off limits. Hit it just right and you might get lucky enough to run the bases and walk on the infield.

Where better to absorb the history of this ball club than in the middle of the Friendly Confines? Learning about the ivy that covers the walls and memorable anecdotes about players and the team as a whole makes this experience one that won't soon be forgotten. An added bonus: personal cameras and video cameras are welcome!

Tweens and Teens Tip: Tours are given on the half hour and cost $25 per person. Space is limited, so it is imperative to purchase tickets on the website to reserve a spot. The proceeds from the tours go to Cubs Care charities, which means that you're performing a good deed while having a great time.

Chicago-West of the Loop

Chicago's diverse West Side is home to Greektown, Little Italy, Pilsen, Ukrainian Village and Humboldt Park, which are just a few of its neighborhoods that were originally built by communities of immigrants. The West Side is off the beaten path for most travelers, especially because some of the areas on the far west have a reputation for having a higher-than-average crime rate. However, it does have sparkling jewels that lure locals and tourists alike, such as the United Center, the UIC Pavilion, and the Garfield Park Conservatory, to name just a few.

Garfield Park Conservatory

300 N. Central Park Avenue
Chicago
(312) 746-5100
www.garfield-conservatory.org

✪

Hours: Daily 9:00 a.m.–5:00 p.m., Wed 9:00 a.m.–8:00 p.m.
Twitter: @gpconservatory

Designed as "landscape art under glass," the Garfield Park Conservatory has been an awe-inspiringly beautiful piece of Chicago for more than 100 years. Located in the East Garfield Park neighborhood on 4.5 acres of land, the Conservatory is made up of six greenhouses (containing spectacular examples of ferns, cacti, palms, and many other specimens), an indoor children's garden, an outdoor 3,000 square foot labyrinth, and more.

Don't miss the annual Chocolate Festival held the week before Valentine's Day, when the staff teaches the origin of this sweet treat. It really does grow on trees! Admittance to the park is always free; during special events, a suggested donation may be posted. There is plenty of free parking on the streets surrounding the park, which makes this one of the best values for families in the city of Chicago.

Tweens and Teens Tip: Interested in horticulture and/or doing something wonderful for the community? The Garfield Park Conservatory has a "Green Teens Program." Over the course of ten weeks, area high school students are trained in leadership, personal, and social development skills as well as post-high school preparedness, and then they can apply what they've learned by working as docents at the Conservatory.

National Museum of Mexican Art
1852 W. 19th Street
Chicago
312-738-1503
www.nationalmuseumofmexicanart.org
✪
Hours: Tues–Sun 10:00 a.m.–5:00 p.m.

The mission of the National Museum of Mexican Art, located in the Pilsen neighborhood, is to spread the understanding that Mexican culture is "sin fronteras" (without borders). The NMMA received accreditation by the American Association of Museums—the only Latino museum to do so—and had to expand in 2001 in order to make more room for its 6,000-piece collection, which is made up of prints, photography, drawings, paintings, sculpture, textiles, and more.

The NMMA has an extensive youth program in place. Radio Arte, the only Latino-owned, youth-driven, urban community radio station in the country, is operated through the museum and offers a one-year, bilingual media-training program. The station seeks to redefine radio for today's audience by spotlighting traditional Latin Alternative music as well as embracing the fusion of Latino music and influence with modern genres. The NMMA educates local youth in the many facets of art and provides internships that help prepare them for a career in the field through its youth initiative, Yollocalli Arts Reach (located nearby).

Tweens and Teens Tip: Heads up, locals: Yollocalli offers free art classes to teenagers. Check their website (www.yollocalli.org) for details and registration information.

United States Post Office Tour

433 W. Harrison Street
Chicago
(312) 983-7550
No website for tours.

✪

Hours: By appointment only; ask for the Manager of Distribution Operations when calling.

The journey that a letter takes from the sender to recipient is more complex than most people can imagine. While e-mail has made snail mail seem quite old-fashioned, there are many occasions on which instantaneous computer technology won't cut it, and so the post office is here to stay.

A tour of the Chicago branch of the United States Post Office is in order if you really want to see what happens after you drop your letter into the big, blue box. (Hint: It doesn't magically appear at its final destination; there's a lot more to it than that!)

The 90- to 120-minute tours are free, and reservations are required. Open-toed shoes, cameras, and large bags are prohibited.

Tweens and Teens Tip: Tours may be discontinued with little notice for security reasons. Call ahead to make sure that you won't be turned away at the door!

Windy City Rollers

525 S. Racine Avenue
Chicago
(312) 413-5740
www.windycityrollers.com
$$$
Hours: Sat 6:00 p.m.–9:00 p.m.
Twitter: @windycityroller

Roller derby, the contact team sport on wheels that was at the height of its popularity in the 1970s and 1980s, has made a comeback in the last couple of years. Bouts (derby matches) are skated by team members who typically wear punk-style outfits and have creative names that can be intimidating or funny. The Windy City Rollers, Chicago's only nationally ranked women's flat track roller derby league, is made up of four home teams (the Double Crossers, The Fury, Hell's Belles, and the Manic Attackers) and a farm team (the Haymarket Rioters). The home season runs from January through June, and the All-Star season follows, ending with the Women's Flat Track Derby Association Championships in November. The Windy City Rollers' All-Stars is made up of the strongest skaters from each team who represent the league on a national level. The Windy City Rollers' B Team, the Second Wind, plays other leagues in the region.

The WCR home bouts are held at the UIC Pavilion, and the atmosphere is raucous, loud, and colorful. Spectators are from all walks of life, and it can be just as fun to watch the people in the seats as it is watching the action on the track. Roller derby is extremely fast-paced. If you're unfamiliar with the rules, you can find lots of information on the WCR website ahead of time as well as on the pre-printed rule cards which are handed out as you enter the Pavilion.

Tweens and Teens Tip: Spending evening at the roller derby can be interactive, because skaters often hang out in the public areas between matches and are more than willing to pose for pictures and chat with fans about the sport and their experiences. The Windy City Rollers are very focused on making the experience fan-friendly, and the more, the merrier: book a group of 15 or more people through the group sales department (perfect for birthday parties or neighborhood get-togethers) and get 40% off the cost of tickets.

Chicago-South of the Loop

Though boundary definitions can vary depending on whom you ask, most believe that the South Side officially begins at Roosevelt Road, where the Loop ends. Lake Michigan and the Indiana state line make up the eastern borders, and it extends to Midway Airport on the west. Though the area has a reputation for being impoverished and crime-infested, in actuality residents range from blue collar (in Pullman, Bridgeport, and Back of the Yards) to the more affluent (in Hyde Park, Kenwood, and Beverly). The South Side, which makes up the largest area of Chicagoland, is home to wonderful museums, architecture, and parks, as well as U.S. Cellular Field (home of the Chicago White Sox) and Soldier Field (home of the Chicago Bears).

Ashland Avenue Swap-o-Rama

4100 South Ashland Avenue
Chicago
(773) 376-6993
www.swap-o-rama.com
$
Hours: Sat-Sun 7:00 a.m.–4:00 p.m. (Indoors & Outdoors),
Tues 7:00 a.m.–2:00 p.m. (Outdoors only),
Thurs 7:00 a.m.–3:00 p.m. (Outdoors only)

Also see Tri-State Swap-o-Rama, Suburbs South and Melrose Park Swap-o-Rama, Suburbs West.

Dat Donut

8249 S. Cottage Grove Avenue
Chicago
(773) 723-1002
www.datdonut.com
$
Hours: 24/6 (Closed Sundays)

It's difficult to find a good donut shop that isn't part of a national chain. Not only that, but the idea of handmade donuts is pretty outrageous in an era full of technological developments to make tasks easier and quicker. Dat Donuts goes against the grain on both counts. Tucked away on the south side and sharing a building with a barbecue joint, this establishment (named "Dat Donut" by the owner in reference to the way small children say "That") cuts, fries, and frosts each delectable ring by hand, selling a couple hundred dozen to customers daily. A second location at 1979 W. 111th Street was opened recently to spread the Dat Donut gospel.

Donut varieties include cake and glazed, along with chocolate, filled, cinnamon, buttermilk, and more. Apple fritters are also available. If donuts aren't your thing, Dat Donut serves ice cream and other treats as well.

Tweens and Teens Tip: Try the "Big Dat," a donut literally as big around as your head. It's just as delicious as its smaller counterparts and costs less than three bucks.

DuSable Museum of African American History
740 E. 56th Place
Chicago
(773) 947-0600
www.dusablemuseum.org
$
Hours: Mon–Sat 10:00 a.m.–5:00 p.m., Sun 12:00 p.m.–5:00 p.m.
Twitter: @dusablemuseum

The mission of the DuSable Museum of African American History is to collect, preserve, interpret, and disseminate the history and culture of Africans and Americans of African descent. The museum was founded in 1961 and has been at its current location in the Hyde Park neighborhood since 1973.

Most of the art pieces, photographs, artifacts, and other memorabilia contained in the museum's collection have been donated by private parties. Permanent exhibits include "Red, White, Blue & Black: A History of Blacks in the Armed Services," "Africa Speaks," and "A Slow Walk to Greatness: The Harold Washington Story." The DuSable also presents temporary exhibits, films, book signings, musical performances, and workshops throughout the year, which are listed on the website.

Tweens and Teens Tip: Print out the self-guided tour from the website to enrich your visit and get a deeper understanding of the exhibits.

Museum of Contemporary Photography

600 S. Michigan Avenue
Chicago
(312) 663-5554
www.mocp.org
✪
Hours: Mon–Wed 10:00 a.m.–5:00 p.m.,
Thurs 10:00 a.m.–8:00 p.m., Fri–Sat 10:00 a.m.–5:00 p.m.,
Sun 12:00 p.m.–5:00 p.m.
(The museum is closed when Columbia College is closed)

As the leading photography museum in the Midwest, the Museum of Contemporary Photography (MoCP) is in a small space located in the Loop at Columbia College. Exhibits rotate often and MoCP is committed to showcasing both established photographers and those who have yet to make a splash.

Tweens and Teens Tip: Though the galleries in the museum contain only temporary exhibits (changed approximately every two months), the entire permanent collection of more than 9,000 works by 1,000 artists is available on the website. Search by artist or title, and register if you want to save what you like in your own online collection.

Museum

Museum of Science and Industry

5700 South Lake Shore Drive
Chicago
(773) 684-1414
www.msichicago.org
$$$$
Hours: Mon–Sat 9:30 a.m.–4:00 p.m., Sun 11:00 a.m.–4:00 p.m.
Twitter: @msichicago

The Museum of Science and Industry (MSI) is difficult to describe in a nutshell because of the diversity of its collection, but suffice it to say it's all about science in every form imaginable. Visitors enjoy the hands-on nature of the museum because learning is made fun. Most native Chicagoans have fond memories of visiting MSI as youngsters, and the museum adds new exhibits regularly to keep fans coming back for more. The very first interactive experience at MSI, the Coal Mine (created in 1933), takes guests to the bottom of a mineshaft as they learn about the work conditions and practices of American miners. The U-505 Submarine, a German vessel that operated of the coast of West Africa in World War II, is a staple for MSI visitors who enjoy the experience of walking onboard this vintage ship and learning the story of its place in history. Another perennial favorite is Colleen Moore's Fairy Castle, an exquisite doll house created and owned by the silent film star in the 1930s. The miniature world inside has delighted MSI visitors since 1949.

Newer permanent exhibits include "You! The Experience," which teaches visitors about the connection between the human body, mind, and spirit as it relates to living a full life, and "Science Storms," an interactive exhibit which explores our understandings of natural phenomena such as hurricanes, tornadoes, tsunamis, lightning, atoms in motion, sunlight, and fire. The museum houses the requisite gift shops, eateries, and a photo studio.

Tweens and Teens Tip: Check out the SciPass opportunities at "You! The Experience." With this innovative tool, visitors can save parts of the exhibits for later. The interview from "Talk to Me" can be recorded and the list of "100 Things To Do" can be saved, just by scanning a SciPass. The information can be retrieved from the museum's website after you go home.

National Vietnam Veterans Art Museum
1801 South Indiana Avenue
Chicago
(312) 326-0270
www.nvvam.org
$$
Hours: Tues–Sat 10:00 a.m.–5:00 p.m.
Twitter: @NVAMChicago

The horrors of war are often indescribable. It is for that reason that art therapy is one of the first steps in the healing process of veterans who are recovering from Post-Traumatic Stress Disorder. The National Vietnam Veterans Art Museum opened in 1981 as the first (and only) museum in the world with a permanent art collection spotlighting the sensitive subject of war.

The NVVAM is the home of more than 1,500 works of art by more than 100 artists. Pieces include paintings, sculpture, photography, poetry, and music. It houses the *Above and Beyond* Memorial, the first new permanent Vietnam memorial (other than The Wall in Washington, D.C.) to contain the names of every person who was killed in action. *Above and Beyond* consists of more than 58,000 imprinted dog tags, hanging from the ceiling of the museum, evenly spaced as if they are soldiers standing in formation.

Tweens and Teens Tip: Various teacher lesson plans for different parts of the museum can be found on the website. Print one out before visiting and use it as a conversation starter to enrich your experience.

New, New Maxwell Street Market

Des Plaines Street and Roosevelt Road
Chicago
312-745-4676
www.explorechicago.org
♦
Hours: Sun 7:00 a.m.–3:00 p.m.

Ahead of its time, the original Maxwell Street Market (which opened in the late 19th century) was a place for any entrepreneur to make money selling whatever he or she wanted. The large, open-air market was full of European immigrants who were buying *and* selling; one of the big draws was the ability to haggle over prices in order to save some money. One hundred years after its inception, the market had to be moved over to Canal Street due to major developments in the neighborhood. In 2008, the New Maxwell Street Market was moved again to its current location, hence the extra "New" in its name.

One thing that hasn't changed over the years is the ability to buy just about anything; in fact, it has been noted that some of the "used" merchandise may have actually been stolen. Beyond that, the New, New Maxwell Street Market is the place to get fresh produce, clothing, tools, jewelry, CDs, and household goods from more than 500 vendors while munching on the best of the best ethnic food in the area.

Tweens and Teens Tip: Bring cash! Haggling is a tradition that stuck over the years, and you can wheel and deal with the vendors to get even better bargains.

Museum

Oriental Institute Museum
1155 E. 58th Street
Chicago
(773) 702-9514
www.oi.uchicago.edu/museum

✪

Hours: Tues 10:00 a.m.–6:00 p.m., Wed 10:00 a.m.–8:30 p.m.,
Thurs–Sat 10:00 a.m.–6:00 p.m., Sun 12:00 p.m.–6:00 p.m.,
Closed Mondays
Twitter: @oimuseum

This museum on the University of Chicago campus in Hyde Park is chock-full of artifacts from the ancient Middle East, but don't be confused by its name: Egypt, Iraq, Iran, Turkey, Israel, Palestine, Sudan, and Syria were referred to as "The Orient" at the beginning of the 20th century. Eight galleries house treasures such as a statue of King Tut, religious artifacts, ancient jewelry, photographs, and much more, all telling the stories of long ago.

Admission is free (donations are suggested), and audio tours are available for a nominal fee to non-members. If you're accompanying history buffs, plan on spending a couple of hours exploring this place, one of Chicago's best-kept secrets.

Tweens and Teens Tip: The museum offers free feature films and documentaries at 2:00 p.m. on Sundays year-round; docents are available afterwards to answer questions. Check the website for current offerings.

Original Rainbow Cone

9233 S. Western Avenue
Chicago
(773) 238-7075
www.rainbowcone.com
$

Hours: Open seasonally from March to November; hours increase throughout the summer. Check website for details.

A Chicago legend that opened its doors in 1926, the Original Rainbow Cone in Beverly is a delectable summer dessert that is worth the drive from anywhere in Chicagoland. Five flavors of ice cream slices are stacked into a cone to make up this frozen feast for the senses: chocolate, strawberry, Palmer House (vanilla with cherries and walnuts), pistachio, and orange sherbet. Of course, there are other options available at this far-south side eatery. You can get a traditional sundae made from your choice of thirty flavors as well as floats, shakes, and other sweet treats.

The Original Rainbow Cone is only open during the summer, so check for current hours before you head out!

Tweens and Teens Tip: Can't make it all the way to Beverly? You can get your rainbow fix at the centrally located Taste of Chicago in Grant Park every summer, and at a location inside the Halsted Street Deli in the Loop (also seasonal)!

Also see Original Rainbow Cone, Chicago Loop.

Robie House

5757 S. Woodlawn Avenue
Chicago
(312) 994-4000
www.gowright.org
$$$
Hours: Tour times vary. Check website for details.
Twitter: @flwpt

Chicago has a very important place in the history of the Prairie style of architecture. One of the best examples is the Robie House, designed by Frank Lloyd Wright (at his Oak Park Studio) in 1908 and built in 1910 at the corner of 58th and Woodlawn. An architectural masterpiece, Robie House features vast amounts of art glass, cantilevered roofs, and one of the first-ever three-car garages. The Robies eventually sold the home in order to pay off family debts. Years later the Chicago Theological Seminary—which had used the home as a dormitory—attempted to have the house demolished. A movement to save the house commenced, and the Robie House was the first building in Chicago to be designated a Chicago landmark.

The University of Chicago has retained ownership of the Robie House for more than thirty-five years. It was opened to the public (by the Frank Lloyd Wright Preservation Trust) in 1997. A massive, ten-year restoration project is being completed at the home, ensuring many more years of public enjoyment. The building has remained open for tours throughout the restoration.

Tweens and Teens Tip: Download an MP3 audio tour of the exterior from the website before visiting. Tours are offered Friday through Sunday from 11 a.m.–3 p.m. Buying tickets in advance is highly recommended. Themed tours of the Robie House are offered on the second Saturday of each month.

Spertus Museum

610 S. Michigan Avenue
Chicago
(312) 322-1700
www.spertus.edu/museum
$$
Hours: Sun 10:00 a.m.–5:00 p.m., Wed 10:00 a.m.–5:00 p.m.,
Thurs 10:00 a.m.–6:00 p.m.
Twitter: @spertus

The Spertus Museum, an offshoot of the Spertus Institute of Jewish Studies, is housed in a beautifully angular glass-front building facing Grant Park and Lake Michigan. The Open Depot collection, which is approximately 1,500 Judaic sculpture and ceremonial objects from different historical periods taken from the museum's master collection of 10,000 objects, is presented in a very modern semi-circular display area. The museum also contains a Holocaust memorial hall in which visitors can reflect on this tragic period in history.

What you see isn't all you get. Because part of the mission of the museum (and the Institute) is to preserve and share artifacts, books, films, music, artwork, maps, and archival items of Jews throughout history, the general public is welcome to conduct research by appointment. Information about the extensive collections held by Spertus is on the website.

Tweens and Teens Tip: Don't bother trying to visit Spertus on Saturdays. The entire building closes early on Friday afternoons through Sunday morning in observance of the Jewish Sabbath.

Food

Tommy Guns Garage

2114 S. Wabash Avenue

Chicago

312-225-0273

www.tommygunsgarage.com

$$$$$

Hours: Wed–Thurs 7:15 p.m. (doors open at 6:00 p.m.), Fri 8:15 p.m. (doors open at 7:00 p.m.), Sat 7:15 p.m. (doors open at 6:00 p.m.), Sun 6:45 p.m. (doors open at 5:30 p.m.). Check the website for Show Days; there are no Wednesday evening shows from October through March.

This dinner theater performance experience set in a 1920s speakeasy begins when you must say the password in order to gain entry. Tommy Gun's Garage is Chicago's longest running audience interactive dinner show, in operation since 1987. The menu includes lasagna, prime rib, pork chops, salmon, and chicken. All choices are served with soup or salad, vegetable, potato, bread, coffee, soft drinks, and dessert.

The musical comedy review after dinner gives the resident gangsters and flappers a chance to entertain the audience. Many audience members even become part of the show, being brought up to the stage to join in on the fun. As with any speakeasy, the danger of being raided by the police is a constant concern, so adults should be ready to hide their hooch (alcohol)!

Tweens and Teens Tip: The website has a great section on 1920s history; read it ahead of time to have greater insight on what's going on. Also online: monthly specials that will bring down the cost of the show!

William Powers State Park

12949 Avenue O

Chicago

773-646-3270

http://dnr.state.il.us/LANDS/landmgt/parks/R2/Wmpow.htm

✪

Hours: 6:00 a.m.–sunset, daily

Picnicking, fishing (summer and winter), boating, and hunting are only a few of the activities visitors to William Powers State Park can enjoy. Wildlife making their home here include a wide variety of fish (largemouth bass, walleye, yellow perch), birds, and "everyday" mammals like squirrels, raccoons, rabbits, and coyotes. Deer sightings have been reported, but they are rare.

In 2002 the park hosted the Calumet BioBlitz, during which scientists and the public worked together for a 24-hour period, inventorying more than 2,200 plant, animal, and micro-organism species alive and well in this region, which is rife with landfills, refineries, and abandoned steel mills.

Tweens and Teens Tip: The park, located along the Illinois/Indiana state line and adjacent to Wolf Lake, is maintained and protected by several community groups who perform semi-annual cleanups, keeping the park visitor-friendly. It's a great way for teens to give back to the community while enjoying the outdoors!

Northern Suburbs

While exploring the northern suburbs of Chicago, you might feel an eerie sense of familiarity. That's because the area has been often used as the settings for many movies (most notably the 1980s films of the late writer/director John Hughes, a resident himself). Some of the most affluent neighborhoods in the United States, let alone Chicagoland, are found in this region, and the cultural, dining, and shopping offerings tend to reflect that.

Chicago Botanic Garden

1000 Lake Cook Road
Glencoe
847-835-5440
www.chicago-botanic.org
✪
Hours: Sun–Sat 8:00 a.m.–sunset
Twitter: @chicagobotanic

No green thumb? You just might want to work on it after you visit the Chicago Botanic Garden! Their mission is "to promote the enjoyment, understanding, and conservation of plants and the natural world." It is one of the country's most-visited public gardens. The Garden is on 385 acres, and its twenty-four display gardens and three native habitats are situated on nine islands surrounded by lakes.

One of the best features of the Chicago Botanic Garden is the diversity offered by the individual gardens. The English Walled Garden is made up of six differently styled garden rooms that are bordered by stone, brick, hedges and trees. The Bonsai Collection features 185 bonsai that are rotated into the collection at their peak time of year. The Sensory Garden is a treat for hands, nose, ears, *and* eyes. To get an overview of all garden areas, pay the small extra fee for the *Grand Tram Tour*, which goes around the perimeter of the Garden. (Also available: the *Bright Encounters Tram Tour*, which focuses on the main island gardens.)

Tweens and Teens Tip: Avid cyclists can ride to the Chicago Botanic Garden on the Chicago Bikeway System, saving the parking fee. Bicycles can be locked up on racks that are located near the parking lots. Once there, take a walk: check the website for conservation walks that are customized by season and Garden area.

Dave's Down to Earth Rock Shop & the Prehistoric Life Museum

704 Main Street
Evanston
(847) 866-7374
www.davesdowntoearthrockshop.com

◆

Hours: Mon, Tues, Thurs, Fri 10:30 a.m.–5:30 p.m.,
Sat 10:00 a.m.–5:00 p.m., Closed Wed and Sun

For decades, young people have made a hobby out of finding colorful stones and — if they're lucky enough to have a rock tumbler — polishing them to display-worthy quality. One such young man turned his hobby into a business by opening Dave's Down to Earth Rock Shop in 1970, with his parents' help. Starting with fossils from Mazon Creek, Dave grew his collection to include rocks, minerals, crystals, and pottery. He is now the go-to guy for these natural treasures, which are available in every price range at his Evanston store.

After browsing the retail store, head downstairs to the Prehistoric Life Museum to get a look at Dave's extensive collection of fossils and bones, along with one of the world's largest dinosaur eggs. Some of the artifacts seen here are three billion years old! Admission to the museum is free.

Tweens and Teens Tip: Make sure to utilize the staff. They are experts who can add depth and information to your experience: all you have to do is ask!

Great Lakes Naval Museum

Building 42, 610 Farragut Avenue
Great Lakes
847-688-3154
www.greatlakesnavalmuseum.org

✪

Hours: Wed–Thurs 1:00-5:00 p.m., Fri 11:00 a.m.–5:00 p.m.,
Sat 1:00-5:00 p.m. Closed on Federal holidays.

The average citizen can't really appreciate what it takes for a young man or woman to survive and thrive during the eight weeks of enlisted training provided by U.S. Navy Boot Camp unless it is personally experienced, but the Great Lakes Naval Museum offers exhibits that enhance the understanding of it. From the Processing Days (P-Days) of week one all the way through the Pass in Review that marks the recruits' graduation and entrance into the fleet at the end of week eight, visitors learn about the mind-boggling amount of preparation that our sailors put in before shipping out.

The museum collection includes photos, uniforms, boot camp flags, vintage recruit magazines, information about Great Lakes Naval Base and its training programs dating back to the 1920s, and oral and written personal histories.

Tweens and Teens Tip: The museum is now located near Gate 1 at Great Lakes Naval Base and visitors no longer need to procure a visitor pass to the base for entry. Group tours are available by appointment.

Holocaust Memorial Foundation

9603 Woods Drive
Skokie
847-967-4800
www.ilholocaustmuseum.org
$$
Hours: Mon–Wed 10:00 a.m.–5:00 p.m., Thurs 10:00 a.m.–8:00 p.m.,
Fri 10:00 a.m.–5:00 p.m., Sat–Sun 11:00 a.m.–4:00 p.m.
Twitter: @ihmec

The horrific killings of six million Jews targeted only because of their religion, political beliefs, or sexual orientation took place in a very dark time in history. To keep something of this magnitude from happening again, it must never be forgotten, and younger generations must be educated. That is the mission of the Holocaust Memorial Foundation, a world-class museum dedicated to preserving the memories of those lost as well as teaching about our responsibility to fight hatred, indifference and genocide.

The facility is architecturally interesting and made up of two halves connected by a hinge. Visitors enter the dark side of the building, which houses exhibits focusing on Hitler's rise to power and the "descent into darkness." The hinge of the building features an early 20th century German rail car, which leads into the second half of the building. It is full of natural light and features exhibits that are centered on the rescue and renewal of Holocaust survivors.

Tweens and Teens Tip: The subject matter can be heavy for visitors of any age. Use the museum as a starting point for some great family discussions about history, human rights, and the future.

Illinois Beach State Park
1 Lake Front Drive
Zion
847-662-4811
http://dnr.state.il.us/LANDS/LANDMGT/
PARKS/R2/ILBEACH.HTM
✪
Hours: Daily 8:00 a.m.–sunset (Nov–Mar),
Daily sunrise-sunset (Apr–Oct)

Summertime brings about the desire to head to the dunes, and Illinois Beach State Park has them. Located in the northeast corner of Illinois, the park runs along Lake Michigan for six miles and features, in addition to the dunes, a beach, wetlands, prairie, and woodlands. The southern end of the park has been designated as a nature preserve.

Boaters, swimmers, hikers, and cyclists descend upon the area as soon as the weather cooperates, and visitors can also camp, with reservations, and fish, with a license. Concessions are available in the main beach area during the summer, but with advanced preparation at home, you can enjoy a great family picnic.

Tweens and Teens Tip: Do your research so you're aware of the restrictions in various areas of the park. For example, bicycles are not permitted on the Dead River or Dunes Trails.

Mitchell Museum of the American Indian

3001 Central Street

Evanston

(847) 475-1030

www.mitchellmuseum.org

$

Hours: Tues–Wed 10:00 a.m.–5:00 p.m., Thurs 10:00 a.m.–8:00 p.m.,
Fri–Sat 10:00 a.m.–5:00 p.m., Sun 12:00 p.m.–4:00 p.m.
Closed Mondays.

Learn about the culture, arts, and history of the Native American Indians at the only Chicago-area museum dedicated to promoting and sharing it. The museum's collection of artifacts from the North American Indian and the Inuit (Eskimo) people dates from the Paleo-Indian period to the present day.

The museum has permanent exhibits focusing on five Native American cultures: the Woodlands, Plains, Southwest, Northwest Coast, and Arctic. The extraordinary craftsmanship of the Native Americans is spotlighted in the vast collections of beadwork, quillwork, pottery, dolls, baskets, carvings, and jewelry. Special temporary exhibits are housed in two galleries that are designated for this purpose.

Tweens and Teens Tip: The museum houses an extensive library of books, periodicals, video, and audiotapes that can be used by visitors who want to learn more.

Par-King Skill Golf

21711 Milwaukee Avenue
Lincolnshire
(847) 634-0333
www.par-king.com
$$
Hours: Vary during spring, summer, and fall (closed winter) and
depend on the weather. Check website for details.

Par-King Skill Golf, home of "America's Most Unusual Golf Courses," came into existence as a place for moms and their children to bide their time while dads shot buckets of balls at the adjacent driving range. (Back then it was called "George's Gorgeous Golfing Gardens.") For more than fifty years, entire families have been spending time practicing their putting on some of the most creative courses in the world.

Each and every course is custom-made (a couple of them have been in use since the beginning!) and hand-painted; when Par-King closes each year for the winter, the elements of each course are refurbished and repainted for the following season. Two of the most popular courses include a replica of the Sears/Willis Tower with a ten-foot-high ball elevator and giant wooden roller coaster that loop-dee-loops. Miniature golf isn't the only game in town, because Par-King is also home to an arcade with video games, pinball, and air hockey.

Tweens and Teens Tip: Due to the complex mechanics of the courses, there is a 48-inch height requirement to enjoy Par-King Skill Golf out of safety considerations. While this can be disappointing to families with younger children, the requirement makes this a truly great place to visit with tweens and teens. Note that Par-King accepts cash only.

Ravinia Festival

200 Ravinia Park Road
Highland Park
(847) 266-5000
www.ravinia.org
$$-$$$$$
Hours: Check website for concert dates and times.
Twitter: @raviniafestival

An evening spent with loved ones under the stars, listening to great music: sounds magical, doesn't it? That element of back-to-basics entertainment is the secret to the success of the Ravinia Festival. Each summer, people of all kinds who share a common love of music visit Ravinia in order to enjoy classic and current artists of many genres, including the Chicago Symphony Orchestra, which makes its summer home there.

Concert seating includes two options: in the pavilion or on the lawn. The pavilion tickets are pricier and offer a view of the stage. Lawn seating, where the view of the stage is completely obstructed, is less expensive and provides an opportunity to partake in the picnic tradition that Ravinia is known for. Food options on-site at Ravinia are plentiful, from fine dining to gourmet-to-go, and there is an ice cream outlet if you forget to bring dessert.

Tweens and Teens Tip: Coming from the city? Take the train to avoid parking headaches. The "Ravinia Special" departs from the Ogilvie Transportation center at festival-friendly times; check the Metra website for schedule and pricing.

Skokie Northshore Sculpture Park

McCormick Boulevard, between Dempster Street and Touhy Avenue

Skokie

(847) 679-4265

www.sculpturepark.org

✪

Hours: 24/7

With more than 60 life-sized sculptures on display, the Skokie North-shore Sculpture Park is the perfect place to enjoy a family picnic, bike ride, or leisurely stroll. The park was created when the Metropolitan Water Reclamation District of Greater Chicago, who owns the two-mile stretch of land, reached out to the public for ideas on what to do with it. The Village of Skokie, who wanted to clean it up and turn it into a recreational park, worked together with a group of citizens interested in displaying sculptures from artists the world over, and the Skokie Northshore Sculpture Park was born in 1988.

The park, open year-round, is fully accessible to those with disabilities, and admission is free. Public and private tours are available; the schedule can be downloaded from the website.

Tweens and Teens Tip: Photo opportunities abound in this park, and the sculptures run the gamut: there's something for everybody! Although each sculpture has a nameplate, some of them are missing or in disrepair. Download the sculpture guide from the website to get more information on the art pieces.

Northwestern Suburbs

The northwest suburbs are diverse in character, from the industrialized sections near O'Hare Airport to the attraction-filled areas near Schaumburg, Des Plaines, and Gurnee to the beautiful natural features of Round Lake and Grayslake. The region is quite spread-out and you'll definitely need a car to navigate it, but consider it! You'll enjoy some of the best features the Chicago suburbs have to offer.

Dad's Slot Cars

700 Lee Street
Des Plaines
(847) 298-0688
www.dadsslotcars.com
$$
Hours: Tues–Sat 12:00 p.m.–8:30 p.m., Sun 12:00 p.m.–5:00 p.m.
Closed Mondays.

These days, the only auto racing that most youngsters are familiar with is that of the video game variety. Slot car racing is old-fashioned, simplistic, repetitive . . . and FUN. At Dad's, guests choose a car to rent and pay for racing time in half hour increments. A little like racing Hot Wheels miniature cars on a larger scale, the object of slot car racing is to get the car around the oval as quickly as possible without it flying off the side.

For those who need a mid-race snack, Dad's has an ice cream counter that offers just the right amount of choices, from plain cones to banana splits, to malts and phosphates.

Tweens and Teens Tip: Dad's will give you 15 free minutes of track time for every "A," so be sure to bring in a report card if you visit during the school year.

Gurnee Mills

6170 W. Grand Avenue
Gurnee
(847) 263-7500
www.gurneemills.com

Hours: Mon–Fri 10:00 a.m.–9:00 p.m., Sat 10:00 a.m.–9:30 p.m.,
Sun 11:00 a.m.–7:00 p.m.
Twitter: @gurneemills

The Simon Property Group, responsible for Bloomington Minnesota's Mall of America, opened Gurnee Mills in 1991 and completely changed shopping in the northwestern suburbs. Rather than creating malls that were little more than an indoor cluster of stores, this company focused on building *destinations*. The design of Gurnee Mills is completely different from the typical modern malls that have a center hub area with spokes shooting out from it like a wheel. The "Z" shape of the building, whether intended or not, keeps shoppers walking past the stores for longer periods of time, because there are no shortcuts: the way back to the car is exactly the way they came in.

Although billed as an "outlet mall," Gurnee Mills is the home to every price range from bargain hunter's paradise to upscale, and everything in between. It houses a twenty-screen movie complex complete with stadium seating where you can catch current movies, as well as two food courts.

Tweens and Teens Tip: If shopping and movie watching isn't enough, check out Rink Side Sports for ice-skating and glow-in-the-dark golf, and MC Speedway for slot car racing.

Shopping

IKEA
1800 E. McConnor Parkway
Schaumburg
(847) 969-9700
www.ikea.com/us
◆

Hours: Sun–Thurs 10:00 a.m.–8:00 p.m.,
Fri-Sat 10:00 a.m.–9:00 p.m.

Also see IKEA, Southern Suburbs.

KeyLime Cove Water Park Resort & Hotel
1700 Nations Drive
Gurnee
(877) 360-0403
www.keylimecove.com
$$$$$
Hours: Mon–Fri 10:00 a.m.–9:00 p.m.,
Sat–Sun 9:00 a.m.–9:00 p.m. (water park)
Twitter: @keylimecove

KeyLime Cove is located near the entrance to Six Flags Great America, but is really a destination in itself. The Key West theme is evident upon first sighting: the outside of the resort is painted in the soft, bright hues of the tropics. The lobby is massive and includes shops like LuLu's Swim Shoppe and Island Hoppers Outfitters, for KeyLime Cove-branded souvenirs and other keepsakes, as well as eateries like The Crazy Toucan. The entrance to the Lost Paradise Water Park, as well as D.W. Anderson's Eatery and Ice Cream Parlor, Anna Chovy's Pizzeria, Leapin' Lizards (art supplies), and the RipTide Reef Arcade are all on the lower level.

Guest rooms and suites accommodate between two and twelve people and are decorated in the same bright tropical theme as the public areas. Room rates include passes for the water park; in fact, park use is restricted to resort guests. KeyLime Cove is a cashless water resort: upon check-in, each guest receives a wristband. The Smart Band wristband grants each wearer water park access. It's also a room key and can be used for any and everything in the resort—vending and game token machines, lockers, concessions, shops, and restaurants—the total amount spent will appear on the final bill at checkout.

Tweens and Teens Tip: Parents can set up pre-funded wristbands for the kids, so they can make their own purchase decisions until the money runs out, eliminating wallet-busting surprises on the room total when packing up to go home.

Show

Laugh Out Loud Theater

601 N. Martingale Road
Streets of Woodfield, Ste. 171
Schaumburg
847-240-0386
www.laughoutloudtheater.com
$$$
Hours: Fri–Sat 7:30 p.m. (Family-friendly performances)
Twitter: @loltheater

Improv comedy has had a revival over the past few years, and now there are several places in Chicagoland where you can find "the funny." The Laugh Out Loud Theater is located right across the street from Woodfield Mall and features performances that mix live action, video, and audience participation.

There is not a bad seat in the house; the theater is in a small space. Patrons who arrive early have a better chance of being seated towards the front of the theater. The cast heavily relies on audience suggestion and participation, and it's best to have some ideas ready! The earlier of the two shows on Friday and Saturday evenings is a family-friendly show, and the latter is for adults.

Tweens and Teens Tip: Laugh Out Loud puts on two-week summer camps for teens with sessions in Improv and Sketch comedy. Participants receive, as a part of camp registration, free tickets to an early evening Laugh Out Loud show.

Long Grove Confectionery Company Factory Tour

333 Lexington Drive
Buffalo Grove
(847) 459-3100
www.longgrove.com/acatalog/factory_tours.html
$
Hours: Tours are given Tuesday–Thursday and Saturdays.
Check website for details.

There's something special about chocolate treats that don't look exactly the same because they've come out of a machine. Long Grove Confectionery Company's handcrafted chocolates are sold in fine stores, online, and, of course, in Long Grove. Chocolate-dipped strawberries, English toffee, giant peanut butter cups, Myrtles (salted nuts, caramel, and chocolate), and more are created at the factory in Buffalo Grove.

One of the few remaining factory tours in the area still open to the public, this one is a treat for the senses. The tour starts in a viewing room with a video about how cacao is grown and processed to become chocolate. From there guests are taken down a long corridor with great window views of the candy kitchens where production and packaging are done, supplemented by video presentations. The tour ends in the factory store, where chocolates galore can be purchased at deep-discount pricing.

Tweens and Teens Tip: Reservations are absolutely required for the weekday tours, but it's not difficult to nab a spot with advance planning. On Saturdays the factory now offers free tours on the hour (no reservations are required), but live production is not guaranteed on the weekend.

McDonald's #1 Store Museum

400 N. Lee Street

Des Plaines

(847) 297-5022

http://www.aboutmcdonalds.com/mcd/our_company/museums

✪

Hours: Open Memorial Day to Labor Day only; call for days/hours.

Twitter: @mcdonaldscorp

Pop culture history lessons are always fun, and taking the family to Des Plaines to see how a McDonald's restaurant looked in the early days definitely fulfills that bill. The #1 Store Museum is a recreation of the very first store, which was originally located just across the street where a modern-day McDonald's franchise is open and thriving.

Visit on a sunny day because the museum is actually an "outside, looking in" experience. The original McDonald's had no seating on the inside; rather, it was a walk-up restaurant. Peer through the windows to check out what the crewmembers (employees) used to wear, what the menu offerings were, and how much it all cost. Walk around to the side and see what it was like for those who worked at the grill in the back of the building, and pay special attention to the milkshake machines. Ray Kroc, the founder of McDonald's, was a milkshake salesman before purchasing his first restaurant. Visitors can also check out the vintage automobiles parked outside right under the original "Speedie" road sign.

Tweens and Teens Tip: If hunger strikes after investigating how this fast food behemoth began, head across the street to enjoy the current menu. Be sure to check out the memorabilia that is on display there, including the sign near the counter that denotes that exact location as the birth of the McDonald's chain.

Medieval Times

2001 N. Roselle Road
Schaumburg
(888) WE-JOUST
www.medievaltimes.com
$$$$$
Hours: Show times vary; check website for details.
Twitter: @medievaltimes

Have you ever wanted to watch some good, old-fashioned 11th century jousting while enjoying a hearty meal? If yes, then Medieval Times is the place for you. Dinner guests are seated at tables that line the arena for viewing ease, and served a hearty, family-style meal (A vegetarian option is available to those who reserve it ahead of time). Don't look for silverware; there is none. In order to enjoy the full medieval experience, you'll be eating with your hands.

The audience is divided into six colored cheering sections; guests in each section root for the knight who wears their color. After dinner, there is plenty of time for souvenir shopping and visiting the stables.

Tweens and Teens Tip: Medieval Times almost always has a coupon out there (in newspapers, mailers, etc.) somewhere. Whether it's "buy one, get one free," "free birthday dinner," or any other miscellaneous offers, it can save you loads of money on the experience.

Muvico Rosemont 18
9701 Bryn Mawr Avenue
Rosemont
(847) 447-1030
www.muvico.com
$$$
Hours: Check website for show times.
Twitter: @muvicorosemont

The city of Rosemont has big plans for building an entertainment, shopping, and dining district, and the Muvico Rosemont 18 is the anchor tenant. The theater screens first-run Hollywood releases and offers special amenities that go above and beyond a typical movie house.

For starters, Muvico was the first company to use Sony Premier 4K digital projection technology, enhancing the visual and audio experience. The seating on the lower level is for General Admission patrons who enjoy oversized plush chairs that recline. Concession choices are expanded at Muvico; in addition to popcorn and candy, guests can enjoy pizza and other "bigger" treats. The upper level is the VIP area, which is more expensive and includes free valet parking and popcorn along with love seats for an at-home style experience. (The VIP level is only for patrons who are 21 and up.)

Tweens and Teens Tip: The Digital Den, Muvico Rosemont's Gaming Lounge, features Playstation 3 and Nintendo Wii games, along with a WI-FI lounge equipped with Sony VAIO computers. Admission is free with the purchase of a movie ticket.

Mystic Waters Family Aquatic Center

2025 Miner Street

Des Plaines

(847) 391- 5740

www.desplainesparks.org/facilities/mystic_waters.asp

$$

Hours: Mon–Fri 11:00 a.m.–9:00 p.m., Sat–Sun 11:00 a.m.–8:00 p.m.

(Summer season)

What better way to stay cool in the summer heat than to visit a water park? Park district water parks are plentiful in the Chicago area, and Mystic Waters, which is operated by the city of Des Plaines, fills with families each summer season. Fun for all ages, the park includes the tween- and teen-friendly Otter's Run, whose two 37-foot water slides are the highest in the area, as well as the Crocodile Cove lazy river.

If you're hungry or thirsty, head over to the Island Café for refreshments. Locker rooms are outfitted with coin-operated lockers to keep your belongings secure.

Tweens and Teens Tip: If you'd rather not buy concessions at the park, get a hand stamp, leave for lunch, and return later. Note that the park may close early if the air temperature goes below 70 degrees or if less than 50 people are using the facility.

Novelty Golf

3650 Devon Avenue
Lincolnwood
(847) 679-9434
www.noveltygolf.com
$$
Hours: Sun–Sat 10:00 a.m.–12:00 a.m. (Memorial Day–Labor Day),
abbreviated hours April–May and September–October

Classic miniature golf courses complete with moving parts-loaded obstacles (and a sense of humor) are tough to find these days. Novelty Golf has been open for sixty years and counting, and has two 18-hole, multi-level courses that are challenging for all ages. The design of the facility is just as it's always been, which means that long-time customers who now bring their children and grandchildren can share the same experience they had in the early days.

Golf isn't the only draw here! Novelty Golf also has batting cages, a game room, and the Bunny Hutch Restaurant where cheeseburgers, hot dogs, fries, and sundaes can satisfy growling stomachs.

Tweens and Teens Tip: Another classic feature of Novelty Golf? They only accept cash: no credit cards. Be prepared! Also, ask about their second game discount.

Prime Outlets at Huntley

11800 Factory Shops Boulevard
Huntley
(847) 669-9100
www.primeoutlets.com

Hours: Mon–Sat 10:00 a.m.–9:00 p.m., Sun 10:00 a.m.–7:00 p.m.

Many people are constantly on the prowl for a bargain, and the joy of the hunt is on maximum display at America's outlet malls. Prime Retail, the developer of the Prime Outlet Malls, assembled some of the most popular upscale and designer companies under one roof to offer shoppers great merchandise below the suggested retail price.

Mall tenants include outlets and factory stores from BCBGMAXAZ-RIA, Calvin Klein, Banana Republic, Gap, Ann Taylor, and Tommy Hilfiger. The mall has a food court, free WI-FI, and an ATM. Save extra money by printing store coupons from the website.

Tweens and Teens Tip: If your family needs an overnighter, check out the "Shop and Stay" packages available on the Prime Outlets at Huntley website, which include a nearby hotel room, breakfast, free use of a local gym, discounts off of Prime Outlets eateries, and a Prime Outlets gift card.

Six Flags Great America & Hurricane Harbor

1 Great America Parkway
Gurnee
(847) 249-4636
www.sixflags.com/greatamerica
$$$$$
Hours: Park is open on the weekends only in late-April, daily May
through August, and weekends only in September and October.
Check website for hours.
Twitter: @sfgreatamerica

Formerly Marriott's Great America, this haven for coaster-enthusiasts is a thrill-a-minute and still growing. The Six Flags franchise takes pride in continually outdoing not only other parks, but also its own, and each summer season typically brings a new and exciting attraction or two. Six Flags Great America is noisy, crowded, and full of rides, shows, and games that could please just about anybody, making it a perfect destination for families with tweens and teens.

Hurricane Harbor, the water park area of Six Flags Great America, contains body-drenching rides that are "thrill-rated" from mild to moderate to max. Showers are available for use, and belongings can be secured in the locker bays located near the Change Room Area.

Tweens and Teens Tip: This amusement park is very costly without the benefit of the various offers that are publicized each season. Soda cans often have a coupon for a nice discount on admission printed on them, and area grocery stores occasionally offer reduced admission as well. Save even more—and get a break from the chaos—by bringing a picnic lunch and eating it at the car after your hand has been stamped for re-entry. For drinks inside the park, buy their sport bottle full of soda. The purchase includes free or reduced-price refills all day, and the bottle can also be filled at the water fountains.

Superdawg

333 S. Milwaukee Avenue
Wheeling
(847) 459-1900
www.superdawg.com

♦

Hours: Sun–Thurs 11:00 a.m.–11:00 p.m.,
Fri–Sat 11:00 a.m.–midnight
Twitter: @superdawgwheel

Also see Superdawg, Chicago-North of the Loop.

Show

Tempel Farms
17000 Wadsworth Road
Wadsworth
847-623-7272
http://www.tempelfarms.com
$$$$
Hours: Sun 1:00 p.m. & Wed 10:30 a.m.

Lipizzaner horses have been selectively bred for more than 400 years for presidents and kings. Over the years, their existence has been threatened by wars and unsatisfactory living conditions. Tempel Farms prides itself on being the only place in the United States where Lipizzans are bred, trained, and perform on-site.

Performances (in the summer only) display the stages the animals go through in their training, starting with mares and foals and ending with the "Ballet of the White Stallions," featuring mature horses. The 70-minute show takes place outdoors unless the area experiences inclement weather; in that case, everything moves indoors. After the show, guests are invited to take a self-guided stable tour.

Tweens and Teens Tip: Tempel Farms offers off-season (October-May) tours by appointment. Visit the stable, watch the trainers work with the horses, and participate in a question and answer session. Minimum group size is five people, and reservations are required.

Volo Auto Museum

27582 Volo Village Road
Volo
(815) 385-3644
www.volocars.com
$$
Hours: Daily 10:00 a.m.–5:00 p.m.
Twitter: @voloautomuseum

While it's fun to attend the annual Chicago Auto Show and see what is on the horizon from the car manufacturers, it's also exciting to take a look back. More than 300 automobiles are displayed on the 30-acre grounds of the Volo Auto Museum, formerly a dairy farm. Browsing the extensive collection is a great way to spend an afternoon, and the selection of antique, show, muscle, and Hollywood cars contained in the five auto showrooms will impress even the toughest audience. The museum management also runs a buy, sell, and trade business in case you want to drive one home!

The Volo Auto Museum hosts an antique and furniture mall and gift shop, as well as a 1950s style food court. Enjoy a meal (or snacks) indoors or outdoors in the shaded picnic grove. The museum holds monthly events, so any time of year is a great time to visit.

Tweens and Teens Tip: Don't miss the "Military Museum and Vehicle" exhibit, which features both operational and restored vehicles of many varieties from World War II all the way through the Vietnam and Iraq Wars.

Western Suburbs

Chicagoland used to have a Wild West of sorts: the western suburbs were mostly made up of farmland. As suburban sprawl took effect in the 20th century, city workers built homes in the west because it was a way to live a commutable distance from the crowds and noise of the downtown area at a more affordable price. Over the past twenty years, towns like Naperville, Aurora, and Oswego have seen a huge boost in residents and businesses built to accommodate their every need. The western suburbs have a great reputation for being a wonderful place to raise a family and have ranked near the top of several prominent "Best Places to Live" lists.

America's Historic Roundhouse

205 N. Broadway Street
Aurora
(630) 892-0034
www.rh34.com

♦

Hours: Mon–Thurs 11:00 a.m.–11:00 p.m.,
Fri–Sat 11:00 a.m.–2:00 a.m., Sun 9:00 a.m.–11:00 p.m.
Twitter: @ahroundhouse

The first phase of the Aurora Roundhouse, a facility for building and repairing cars for the Chicago, Burlington and Quincy Railroad, was constructed in 1856. At that time, it was made of twenty-two stalls. Over the next eight years, a total of eighteen stalls were added, making the Roundhouse a complete circle. Improvements and additions to the facility and the buildings around it took place for the next several decades until 1960, when railroad service greatly declined and the facility was no longer needed.

After being empty for thirty years, NFL Hall of Famer and Chicago Bear Walter Payton petitioned the city to redevelop the Roundhouse, and it reopened in 1996 as a 70,000 square foot entertainment complex, housing a restaurant, bar, comedy club, microbrewery, and the Walter Payton Museum, where fans can pay homage to "Sweetness" and take a look at memorabilia from his life and career.

Tweens and Teens Tip: The Roundhouse microbrewery produces Roundhouse Root Beer in small batches every six weeks. Purchase some to take home in three sizes: bottles, Pony Barrels, and Half Barrels!

American Science & Surplus

33W361 Route 38
Geneva/West Chicago
(630) 232-2882
www.sciplus.com
♦

Hours: Mon–Wed 10:00 a.m.–7:00 p.m.,
Thurs 10:00 a.m.–8:00 p.m., Fri 10:00 a.m.–7:00 p.m.,
Sat 10:00 a.m.–6:00 p.m., Sun 11:00 a.m.–5:00 p.m.
Twitter: @sciplus

See American Science & Surplus, Chicago-North of the Loop.

Zoo

Brookfield Zoo
8400-31st Street
Brookfield
(708) 688-8000
www.brookfieldzoo.org
$$$
Hours: Seasonal; check website for details. Zoo is open year-round.
Twitter: @brookfield_zoo

Managed by the Chicago Zoological Society, Brookfield Zoo has been around since 1934 and has been visited by millions of Chicago children on school field trips over the years. The zoo is huge and is the home to more than 400 species. The list of permanent exhibits is extensive. Favorites include the "Australia House," "Habitat Africa," and "The Living Coast."

Though the general admission pass includes most of what the zoo has to offer, two upgrades are available if your family is interested in experiencing attractions like the Dolphin Show, Stingray Bay, and the Carousel. From spring through fall, the zoo offers a Motor Safari, on which you can take a narrated tour of the entire zoo. Many dining options are available on the grounds, or if you'd rather bring a picnic, that's allowed here.

Tweens and Teens Tip: Start your zoo adventure even before you get there by taking the train: Metra's Burlington Northern line has a Zoo Stop (Hollywood Station). From there, walk six blocks northeast to the zoo entrance.

Cantigny Gardens & Park

1S151 Winfield Road
Wheaton
630-668-5161
www.cantigny.org
$
Hours: Daily 9:00 a.m.–sunset (March–April), Daily 7:00 a.m.–sunset
(May–October), Daily 9:00 a.m.–sunset (November–December),
Fri-Sun 9:00 a.m.–sunset (February) (These are hours for the
grounds; check the website for attraction hours.)
Twitter: @cantignypark

The official mission of this 500-acre park on land given to the state of Illinois in the 1930s by Chicago Tribune owner Colonel Robert R. McCormick (the park is still a member of his McCormick Foundation) is to offer opportunities for display of and education about Midwestern plants of all varieties, but they're getting much more than that done. There are twenty-two breathtakingly beautiful gardens on the grounds, but if you only go to see the gardens, you'll miss many other fabulous features.

The country home of Colonel McCormick and his first wife Amy is now open to the public as the Robert R. McCormick Museum. Guided tours through the home teach visitors about the family's daily life as well as McCormick's career and his impact on politics and media. The First Division Museum is also located on the grounds of Cantigny, and its mission is to preserve, interpret, and present the history of the 1st Infantry Division. Young people love Tank Park, home of tanks and artillery pieces from World War I through Desert Storm and Desert Shield. Cantigny visitors can also golf on the public, 27-hole course, go bird watching, attend concerts, and dine at one of the four restaurants.

Tweens and Teens Tip: Junior (ages 8–15) golfers can enjoy the 9-hole Youth Links course with their favorite adult. Don't miss the Idea Garden, full of whimsical designs that young people love.

Show

Cascade Drive-In
1100 E. North Avenue
West Chicago
(630) 231-3150
www.cascadedrivein.com
$$
Hours: Check website for show times.

Drive-in movies were all the rage in the mid-20th century. Your family can have a taste of this 1950s phenomenon at one of the country's few remaining drive-in theaters. For an authentic experience, listen to the feature films through the provided in-car speakers. If you're all about modern convenience, the sound comes through on radio station 88.5. Music from the 50s is played before the first movie begins, and commercials from the era that entice the purchase of movie snacks are screened during intermission.

The Cascade has one screen but always offers a double feature. The offerings are changed regularly, and the bonus for visitors is that the admission price includes both movies. The theater is open on summer weekends and accepts cash only. There is a full-service food concession but food from home is permitted. You can even bring charcoal and use their grills to cook up some burgers or dogs.

Tweens and Teens Tip: During the second film, the management sometimes offers a $1 sale on all concession items. Also, ask about their Frequent Movie Bonus Card, which can be exchanged for a free carload admission after six visits.

Chicago Premium Outlets

1650 Premium Outlets Boulevard

Aurora

630-585-2200

www.premiumoutlets.com

♦

Hours: Mon–Sat 10:00 a.m.–9:00 p.m., Sun 10:00 a.m.–6:00 p.m.

Twitter: @premiumoutlets

Designed to be an outdoor-style mall where all stores open up to a partially covered (but not completely enclosed) walkway outside, the Chicago Premium Outlets Mall is best enjoyed on warm and breezy days, but is sheltered enough for year-round excursions.

Brand names represented here vary widely and include Swarovski, Le Creuset, Kate Spade, Coach, Nike, Crocs, Gap, Tommy Hilfiger, Salvatore Ferragamo, Juicy Couture, Sony, and many more. In all, over 120 retailers make their home here. The mall has a large food court, as well as a Starbucks. Sweet offerings such as Rocky Mountain Chocolate Factory, Godiva Chocolatier, and Lindt Chocolate keep energy levels high.

Tweens and Teens Tip: The mall has huge holiday sales on the weekends of Memorial Day, July 4th, Labor Day, Columbus Day, Thanksgiving, and Christmas weekends. Hours are extended, and discounts are plentiful. Check the website for current store specials and sign up for the VIP Shopper Club for exclusive discounts.

The Comedy Shrine
4034 Fox Valley Center Drive
Aurora
(630) 585-0300
www.comedyshrine.com
$$$$
Hours: Sat 4:00 p.m. (by teens, for teens) & 6:00 p.m. (for families
with children ages 6–16), Fri–Sat 8:00 p.m. (for ages 14 and up)

Upon arrival at The Comedy Shrine, visitors immediately discover
where the theater got its name. Owner Dave Sinker's massive collection of comedy memorabilia (posters, headshots, dolls, figurines,
lamps, clocks . . . you name it!) is on display, museum-style, in the lobby.
The theater moved to its current Aurora location in the spring of 2011
after a five-year stint in downtown Naperville.

The talented members of the adult improv troupe come from well-
known comedy playgrounds such as Second City, ComedySportz,
Improv Olympics, and Annoyance Theater. Due to the pace and
unpredictability of improvisational comedy, the performers seem to
have just as much fun performing as the audience has watching. Reservations are highly recommended for all shows. If your family is part
of another group, the ticket office needs to know ahead of time so
they can make sure everyone is seated together. There is a one-drink
minimum. (Though alcohol is served, water and soft drinks count, too.)

Tweens and Teens Tip: The Comedy Shrine offers Improv Boot
Camp during the summer for young people (ages 8–17) and classes for
teens year-round. Graduates of the teen classes perform on Saturdays
at 4:00 p.m. for a teenaged audience.

Cookie Dough Creations

22 W. Chicago Avenue

Naperville

(630) 369-4833

www.cookiedoughcreations.com

$

Hours: Mon–Thur 10:00 a.m.–9:00 p.m., Fri 10:00 a.m.–10:00 p.m., Sat 12:00 p.m.–10:00 p.m., Sun 12:00 p.m.–9:00 p.m.

(Open one hour later May–August)

Cookie dough lovers can finally stop worrying about the risks of salmonella and start rejoicing! Nestled in Downtown Naperville is the only known establishment—on the planet!—that specializes in a safe-to-eat, egg-free version of this treat. Once featured on Food Network's "Roker on the Road," this sweet spot caters to fans of all ages. Families visiting the Naperville Riverwalk area have rested their feet and treated their taste buds in this cozy shop—whose walls are decorated with a colorfully painted mural and menu—since 1995.

Not a cookie dough fan? *No problem*: Cookie Dough Creations serves up freshly baked cookies as well as ice cream, cheesecake, brownies, and other frozen goodies. Hard-core dessert fans can enjoy a Cookie Dough Sundae, which is a bowl of ice cream topped with cookie dough!

Tweens and Teens Tip: The inexpensive menu and Chicago Avenue location makes this eatery a perfect place to either enjoy after dinner or as a stand-alone date!

Danada Equestrian Center
3S503 Naperville Road
Wheaton
630-668-6012
www.danada.info/
♦

Hours: Vary according to program; check website for details.
Twitter: @dupageforest

The mission of the Danada Equestrian Center is to provide visitors with an equestrian program that is both educational and recreational, and they've been doing just that for nearly thirty years. Assisted by volunteers, the professional staff offers classes, trail rides, seminars, and camps. There's something for everybody here.

Those who want to learn as much as possible about horses can sign up for Horsemanship classes (they offer five levels); no experience is required to sign up for Horsemanship I. One-hour trail rides, led by the staff, are available for those who have completed Horsemanship I or a placement exam. The rides must be purchased in packages of six and are available from April through November on Fridays, Saturdays, and Sundays. If the idea of riding a horse isn't as exciting as the idea of being pulled in another form of transport by one, 30-minute public horse-drawn hayrides are offered, as are 15-minute sleigh rides.

Tweens and Teens Tip: Various summer camps are offered for local teens, and if you're really serious about horses (and are at least fourteen years old), sign up for their great volunteer program that provides hands-on knowledge of horses and their care.

Elmhurst Art Museum

150 Cottage Hill Avenue
Elmhurst
(630) 834-0202
www.elmhurstartmuseum.org
$
Hours: Tues–Thurs 10:00 a.m.–5:00 p.m., Fri 10:00 a.m.–8:00 p.m.,
Sat 10:00 a.m.–5:00 p.m. (Closed Sun–Mon)

Robert H. McCormick couldn't have imagined in his wildest dreams that the home he had built in the 1950's would live a second life as a major part of the city of Elmhurst. The home, known as McCormick House and designed by German-American architect Mies van der Rohe, was moved to Wilder Park in 1994 where the brick, glass, and steel masterpiece would become the heart of the Elmhurst Art Museum.

The museum itself, named "The Best Suburban Art Museum in Chicago" by Chicago Magazine, features 20th century art in various forms by Illinois, regional, and national artists. It is located adjacent to the Elmhurst Public Library and across Wilder Park from the Lizzadro Museum of Lapidary Art.

Tweens and Teens Tip: Young visitors (ages twelve and younger) are admitted free daily, but everybody gets free admission on Tuesdays. The museum offers some great workshops and camps for tweens and teens in conjunction with the Elmhurst Park District.

Museum

Farnsworth House
14520 River Road
Plano
630-552-0052
www.farnsworthhouse.org
$$$$
Hours: Tues–Sun 10:00 a.m.–3:00 p.m.
(April–November only), Closed Mondays.
Twitter: @miesglasshouse

Ludwig Mies van der Rohe, one of the most prominent architects of the 20th century, originally built this minimalistic, steel-and-glass one-room home on the Fox River for Dr. Edith Farnsworth in 1950. The house is glassed-in all around, seamlessly blending in with the landscape outside, the trees and grass becoming a natural extension of the design of Mies van der Rohe.

Tours are approximately 90 minutes long and take visitors (age 12 and up) around the exterior as well as the interior of the house. Though tickets can be purchased at the house, it's best to purchase online rather than making the drive only to find that the day's tours are sold out. The calendar on the website is updated regularly to reflect when tours sell out, which is helpful to know when planning a visit. Bring a camera, but only for the exterior and shots of the interior through the glass. Photography is prohibited while inside the house on the regular public tours. For interior photography clearance, reserve a spot on a Photography Tour, which is more expensive.

Tweens and Teens Tip: Plan to arrive approximately 30 minutes before the start time of a tour, because you must walk approximately a quarter mile on a trail from the parking lot to the house. You will be asked to remove your shoes for the interior portion of the tour.

Fermilab

Pine Street
Batavia
(630) 840-3000
www.fnal.gov

✪

Hours: Vary. Check website for details.
Twitter: @fermilabed

Fermi National Accelerator Laboratory (Fermilab) specializes in high-energy particle physics and is run by the U.S. Department of Energy. Just a few of the great things accomplished there are treating cancer with particle beams, working with electric currents and magnets, and finding new ways to make the elements of technology smaller and more efficient.

Fermilab can be experienced a few different ways. Public tours are conducted on Wednesdays at 10:30 a.m.; reservations are required and participants must be ten years and older. Ask-a-Scientist tours are conducted on the first Sunday of each month. Private tours by appointment are also given to high school-aged (and older) visitors. Groups of six or more students in grades 6-8 can enjoy hands-on science exhibits at the Lederman Science Center at various times, six days per week.

Tweens and Teens Tip: Because the U.S. Government runs Fermilab, national security changes may affect your visit. Be sure to click "Current Status of Access to Fermilab" under the Tours and Programs header on the website before leaving home. Also, don't miss checking out the herd of buffalo on campus. Fermilab's first director, Robert Wilson, brought the first bison on site in 1969 to symbolize Fermilab's connection to the prairie heritage, and they've been a fixture ever since!

Five Star Indoor Swap Mart

300 W. North Avenue
Villa Park
630-835-2800
www.5starswapmart.com

✪

Hours: Mon 12:00 p.m.–7:00 p.m., Wed–Fri 12:00 p.m.–7:00 p.m.,
Sat–Sun 10:00 a.m.–6:00 p.m.

If the journey is just as fun for your family as the destination, spending some time at one of Chicagoland's largest flea markets will be quite the experience. Located in Villa Park, the Five Star Indoor Swap Mart is open in summer and winter, providing an opportunity to browse new merchandise offered by hundreds of merchants at a discounted price.

Admission and parking are free, which leaves plenty of money to buy handbags, jewelry, clothing, home décor, toys, candy, gifts, and more, all offered underneath one climate-controlled roof.

Tweens and Teens Tip: If you're lucky, you might find yourself shopping when live entertainers are there, too. Don't want to leave it to chance? Call for the entertainment schedule!

Fox River Trolley Museum
361 S. LaFox Street
South Elgin
(847) 697-4676
www.foxtrolley.org
$
Hours: Sat 11:00 a.m.–5:00 p.m. (June–Labor Day),
Sun 11:00 a.m.–5:00 p.m. (May–November)

Back in the "olden days" the electric trolley car was a common form of transportation in the United States. You can experience this vanishing slice of Americana firsthand on a four-mile trip along the Fox River banks and through the Jon J. Duerr Forest Preserve.

The tour takes passengers along tracks that once linked Carpentersville, Elgin, Aurora, and Yorkville, and includes the viewing and inspection of many antique trolleys that had their heyday from 1891 to 1952. Trolleys only run during the summer on weekends and some holidays.

Tweens and Teens Tip: Bring a sack lunch to enjoy at one of the picnic tables at the Museum or in the Jon Duerr Forest Preserve. Halloween and Christmas tours are available, and families can enjoy Trolleyfest each August.

Frank Lloyd Wright Home & Studio Tour

951 Chicago Avenue
Oak Park
(708) 848-1976
www.gowright.org
$$$
Hours: Check website for tour schedule.
Twitter: @flwpt

One of the most famous and influential American architects, Frank Lloyd Wright conceptualized a building style that emphasized horizontal lines and blending architecture with the surrounding environment. Though he never attended architecture school, he studied in Chicago under the great Louis Sullivan during the early days, taking Sullivan's belief that "form follows function" and adopting his own version of it, "form and function are one."

Visitors to the Wright Home & Studio can see firsthand where he spent the first twenty years of his career, and more importantly, the birthplace of his Prairie style of architecture. Knowledgeable docents lead tour groups through the breathtakingly restored rooms, showing off the talent of a mind that was very much ahead of its time.

Tweens and Teens Tip: A tour highlight is definitely the Children's Room (Wright raised six children in this house with his first wife, Catherine), complete with a baby grand piano installed so that only part of it takes up room space (the back end is cantilevered outside of the room, over the stairs), oak fretwork light screens, and a Giannini mural. Tours have limited space, so purchasing tickets online is the best way to make sure that you get the date and time you prefer. Themed tours of the home and studio as well as walking tours of the other area homes designed by Wright are also available.

Kane County Cougars

34W002 Cherry Lane
Geneva
(630) 232-8811
www.kccougars.com
$$-$$$
Hours: Check website for game schedule.
Twitter: @kccougars

Taking the family to a major league baseball game is usually a great experience and lots of fun, but there's no denying that it can put a huge dent in the family finances. A great alternative is a minor league game. The Kane County Cougars, a Class A affiliate of the Oakland A's, is a team chock-full of great talent. Part of the excitement of a game is that you might be watching a future major leaguer.

In addition to the ample—and free—parking and the lower-than-the-majors cost of admission (seats on the grass are available for as little as $8 per person!), the benefits of attending a minor league game are many. Giveaways, between-inning entertainment, and autograph sessions are part of the fun as well as post-game fireworks and the running of the bases. The team calendar is packed with regular mascots and entertainers such as Jake the Diamond Dog, Myron Noodleman, Zooperstars, and the Jesse White Tumblers.

Tweens and Teens Tip: Once each season, the Cougars offer a Family Campout at Elfstrom Stadium. Fans pitch a tent at the ballpark after an evening game and camp out overnight. A full-length movie is shown on the big screen in center field, and breakfast is served the next morning.

Kane County Flea Market
525 S. Randall Road
St. Charles
(630) 377-2252
www.kanecountyfleamarket.com
♦

Hours: Sat 12:00–5:00 p.m., Sun 7:00 a.m.–4:00 p.m.
(First weekend of each month ONLY)

One man's trash is another man's treasure: that's the idea behind the grand tradition of flea markets worldwide. The Kane County Flea Market originated in the late 1960s and since then has become one of the most well known in the country. Held at the Kane County Fairgrounds on the first weekend of every month (except January and February), the entrance fee is very reasonable and the parking is free.

The great thing about a flea market is that you can have fun whether you're searching for something specific or just browsing to find the special something you didn't even know you wanted. The booths of nearly 1,000 dealers contain antiques, crafts, collectibles, and new merchandise, and food is available too!

Tweens and Teens Tip: To add an extra element of fun to your treasure hunt, attend the Kane County Flea Market Overnighters (see website for dates). They begin at 4:00 p.m. on a Saturday and end at 2:00 a.m. on Sunday.

Lizzadro Museum of Lapidary Art
220 Cottage Hill Avenue
Elmhurst
(630) 833-1616
www.lizzadromuseum.org
$
Hours: Tues–Sat 10:00 a.m.–5:00 p.m., Sun 1:00 p.m.–5:00 p.m.
(Closed Mondays & major holidays)
Twitter: @lizzadromuseum

Any kid who has a rock tumbler could be considered an amateur lapidary; a lapidary is a craftsman (or woman) who cuts, engraves, and polishes stones. The Lizzadro Museum in Elmhurst's Wilder Park is home to many beautiful creations from the world over, originally collected by Joseph F. Lizzadro Sr., an Italian immigrant who enjoyed the art and wanted to share it with the public.

The upper level of the museum features lapidary art from the Ming Dynasty as well as lapidary dioramas depicting different nature scenes, Chinese ivory puzzle spheres, mosaics, and many more examples of the beauty that can be created with stone. The lower level houses the gift shop and exhibits that are more science-focused, including mineral and fossil displays, miniature minerals that can be viewed through a microscope, and a map of Illinois showing where various rocks and minerals are found.

Tweens and Teens Tip: The museum hosts interesting temporary exhibits on the upper level, and sometimes the pieces on display are for sale. Visit the museum on Fridays for free admission.

Fun & Games

Lost Mountain Adventure Golf

1535 75th Street
Woodridge
(630) 985-9860
www.ziegfieldtroygolf.com
$$
Hours: Vary. Check website for details.

This three-tiered miniature golf course is visible from busy 75th Street and its adventure-themed holes beckon fun-seekers of all ages and skill levels. A subsidiary of Ziegfield Troy Golf Center (located on the same grounds), Lost Mountain features eighteen holes, a 22-foot waterfall, and many twists and turns on every journey from start to finish.

Miniature golf is an inexpensive way to spend an afternoon; unfortunately, this is not a secret. Call the facility to find out when the slower times are if you want to have a leisurely game without letting others play through. During the school year, Lost Mountain stays open later, and yes, it is lighted for night play!

Tweens and Teens Tip: At Hole #7, "Ride the Rapids." If you put the ball into the water on purpose, there's a great chance you'll get a hole in one!

Mayslake Peabody Estate
1717 31st Street
Oak Brook
630-850-2363
www.mayslakepeabody.com
$
Hours: Check the website for details.
Twitter: @dupageforest

Mayslake Hall, a Tudor Revival-style mansion, was built by the Marshall and Fox architectural firm at the request of Francis Stuyvesant Peabody, a man who was both the owner of one of the largest coal companies in the United States and an active politician with the Democratic Party. Peabody intended Mayslake to be the country home for him and his family; unfortunately he died one year after it was completed.

After Peabody's death, the family sold the estate to the Franciscan Order, and that organization built the Portiuncula Chapel, which is a replica of its namesake in Assisi, Italy. Currently, the estate is owned and operated by the Forest Preserve District of DuPage County, and tours of Mayslake Hall and Portiuncula Chapel are given to the public year-round with the exception of mid-December through mid-January.

Tweens and Teens Tip: The Mayslake Peabody Estate hosts many events, classes, and lectures on the grounds. Offerings include sessions such as native plant sales, hikes, photography and gardening classes, theater, dance, and much more. Up-to-date information can be found on the Events Calendar on the website.

Melrose Park Swap-o-Rama

4600 W. Lake Street

Melrose Park

(708) 344-7300

www.swap-o-rama.com

$

Hours: Sat–Sun 7:00 a.m.–4:00 p.m. (Indoors & Outdoors),
Fri 8:00 a.m.–3:00 p.m. (Outdoors only)

Also see Tri-State Swap-o-Rama, Southern Suburbs and Ashland Avenue Swap-o-Rama, Chicago-South of the Loop.

Morton Arboretum

4100 Illinois Route 53
Lisle
(630) 968-0074
www.mortonarb.org
$$
Hours: Daily 7:00 a.m.–sunset
Twitter: @mortonarb

The Morton Arboretum, an outdoor museum of sorts, contains thousands of trees and other plants that are grown as much for propagation and research as they are for the enjoyment of visitors. As would be expected in 1700 acres of living materials, the scenery is always changing and multiple visits are encouraged, to take advantage of the entire facility and all its parts.

Features of the Arboretum include the Children's Garden, the Maze Garden, the Thornhill Education Center, the Acorn Express tram, the Gingko Restaurant, the Fragrance Garden, and much more. Visitors can bike, run, hike, ski, and snowshoe on the grounds.

Tweens and Teens Tip: The Morton Arboretum is open 365 days per year. If you live locally, consider joining. The membership cost for a family of four will pay for itself after only three visits and also includes great benefits like one guest pass per visit, a subscription to *Seasons* member publication, various discounts, and reciprocal privileges with more than two hundred other arboreta.

Museum

Naper Settlement

523 S. Webster Street
Naperville
(630) 420-6010
www.napersettlement.org
$$
Hours: Tues–Sat 10:00 a.m.–4:00 p.m.,
Sun 1:00-4:00 p.m. (April–October),
Tues–Fri 10:00 a.m.–4:00 p.m. (November–March)

Smack-dab in the middle of downtown, this living history museum tells the story of how Naperville grew from a 19th century farming village into a bustling town at the turn of the 20th century. Costumed villagers educate visitors in such a way that no two visits are the same.

Tours—which include hands-on activities—begin at the Pre-Emption House, which was the first hotel and tavern west of Chicago, and continue through other buildings such as the Firehouse, century Memorial Chapel, Paw Paw Post Office, Copenhagen Schoolhouse, and more. The grounds themselves are also something to see. Local gardening groups volunteer themselves to maintain the landscaping according to the Master Landscape Plan.

Tweens and Teens Tip: Naper Settlement has four annual events that are well known throughout the area, enrich the experience of a visit, and are great for families: Civil War Days (third weekend in May), Naper Days (Father's Day weekend in June), All Hallows Eve (late October), and Christmas Memories (in December). From November through March, the building interiors are closed to the public. Self-guided audio tours of the grounds and Visitor's Center (with a changing exhibit hall) are included with admission.

Naperville Ghost Tours

36 S. Washington Street
Naperville
630-205-2664
www.naperville-ghosts.com
$$$$$

Hours: Tours are generally on the weekends (Spring through Fall) at 8:00 or 9:00 p.m. You can choose from three tour times on All Hallows Eve and Halloween Night. Check the website for details.

The campus of North Central College, along with the historic district of downtown Naperville, is the setting for Paranormal Investigator, Historian, and Author Kevin Frantz's Naperville Ghost Tours. For a period of 90–120 minutes, Kevin leads groups of up to thirty people on a ghost-hunting excursion that is both fascinating and spooky.

Tours begin and end in Central Park on Washington Street near a free public parking garage. Cameras are allowed, and those who want to enhance their experience by using professional tools can borrow ghost-hunting gear like EMF meters, non-contact thermometers, and infrared video cameras. The minimum age for the tours is thirteen, and tours go on no matter the weather.

Tweens and Teens Tip: To save money, make sure there are five people in your party: the fifth person's admission is only $10. If you want to spend more money, make a reservation for a private ghost tour that you can enjoy from the comfort of a pedicab! (See the website for more information.)

Tour

Naperville Trolley & Tours

Corner of Jackson Avenue and Webster Street
Naperville
(630) 420-2223
www.napervilletrolley.com
$$
Hours: Tours run at 11:00 a.m. on Fridays (June–August only)
Twitter: @napervltrolley

Touring Naperville is more fun when riding a trolley. These unique vehicles are popular choices for transporting guests during a wedding, bar mitzvah, or corporate outings, but you don't have to be an event participant to enjoy a ride. Tours of Naperville are offered weekly during the summer. Attractions include North Central College, the Riverwalk, Naper Settlement, the historic district, and more.

During the winter, the trolley takes passengers on the *December Holiday Light Tour*. Private tours are offered for groups of 21–32 passengers (the trolley will pick the group up at a pre-arranged location), and public tours are also offered by reservation only (the public trolley stop is on Jackson Avenue at Eagle Street).

Tweens and Teens Tip: The drivers are very knowledgeable about Naperville, but if they can't answer a question on the spot they might find the information later and post it on their website. One more thing: if you ask the driver nicely, he or she might let you clang the bell!

Oberweis Dairy Tour

951 Ice Cream Drive

North Aurora

(630) 801-6100

www.oberweisdairy.com/web/tours.asp

$

Hours: Mon & Wed only, 10:00 a.m.

Twitter: @oberweisdairy

Although they still deliver glass bottles of milk directly to your door just like they have since 1927, Oberweis Dairy has expanded its empire to include retail stores (with ice cream counters) area wide, and a tour located at the Dairy itself. Visitors watch a video presentation on the Oberweis story, the farms where their cows live, the life of an Oberweis milkman, and the production and bottling process. Though visitors aren't able to set foot in the actual production area, a large window is available for a behind-the-scenes peek.

The tour ends in the Oberweis Retail Store where you can shop to your heart's content and enjoy a free cup of Oberweis ice cream.

Tweens and Teens Tip: Tours are conducted for groups of between ten and thirty people only, making this a great multi-family activity. Because of the group requirement, reservations are mandatory. Tour participants must be at least eight years old.

Crafting

The Place to Bead

424 Fort Hill Drive, Ste. 102
Naperville
(630) 416-BEAD
www.theplacetobead.com

◆

Hours: Tues–Wed 11:00 a.m.–6:00 p.m., Thurs 11:00 a.m.–7:00 p.m.,
Fri–Sat 11:00 a.m.–5:00 p.m. (Closed Sun–Mon)

Whether making a gift for yourself or for someone else, selecting and hand-stringing small beads is a relaxing way to get your creative juices flowing. Common projects include earrings, bracelets, and necklaces but are only limited to your range of imagination.

If you're a newbie, let the staff know and they will set you up with a tray, a pencil, and a printed slip of paper to keep track of what you're using. They will help determine how long your wire should be — it depends on the project — and will recommend which bead areas you should start with when making selections. Once everything is strung on the wire, the staff will double-check it and finish it securely if you don't know how.

Tweens and Teens Tip: Beading shops are great fun for any budget because you only pay for what you use. Substitutions can be made as you build a project, in order to stay within the limits of your wallet. Classes and parties are offered year-round.

Pottery Bayou
117 Water Street
Naperville
(630) 718-9823
www.pottery-bayou.com

♦

Hours: Sun 12:00 p.m.–5:00 p.m., Tues 11:00 a.m.–7:00 p.m.,
Wed 11:00 a.m.–8:00 p.m., Thurs 11:00 a.m.–7:00 p.m.,
Fri 11:00 a.m.–8:00 p.m., Sat 10:00 a.m.–5:00 p.m.
(Mon by appointment)

This isn't your mom's ceramic shop! The days of painting green ware in a dirty, dusty, warehouse-like room full of metal shelves loaded with plates, mugs, and animal statues are over. Today's ceramic shop is bright, colorful, and clean (well, maybe there's a little dust), and a great place to create that special keepsake. Pottery Bayou is located in downtown Naperville on the Riverwalk, a lovely setting for budding artists.

The cost of your visit is determined by the pottery piece(s) you choose, and there is a studio fee, which covers two hours of paint and studio usage. When you are finished, leave your pottery to be fired, pick it up seven to ten days later, and enjoy!

Tweens and Teens Tip: Studio fees are half off on Tuesdays at Pottery Bayou. Party packages are available, including an option where they come to you (Additional fee for outside of the Naperville area).

Rainbow Falls Water Park

200 Reverend Morrison Boulevard
Elk Grove Village
(847) 228-2860
www.elkgroveparks.org/rainbowfalls.asp
$$$
Hours: Vary. Check website for details.

This tropical-themed water park is part of the Elk Grove Park District and is full of features that will please just about everybody. There's a lazy river and a tot pool, but the older kids will probably spend most of their time on the slides. The Calypso Twist is made up of four body slides, and the Pelican Plunge is a slide that leads to a giant circular bowl before dropping into the pool below.

You're bound to get hungry; recharge with a meal at Hide Away Café. If you want to save some money, pack a picnic. The park has two areas available for just that purpose, Mango Grove and Coconut Grove.

Tweens and Teens Tip: Elk Grove Park District residents not only pay lower admission than non-residents, but also get to enter the park 30 minutes before everybody else. Season passes are available.

Tivoli Theatre

5021 Highland Avenue
Downers Grove
(630) 968-0219
www.classiccinemas.com
$
Hours: Check website for show times.

Did you know that the country's second theatre especially for screening "talkies" (the first movies with sound) was built in the western suburbs of Chicago? The Tivoli opened on Christmas Day 1928 to an around-the-block crowd of 4000 excited moviegoers. It had one very large screen and a stage big enough for vaudeville or other small productions, as well as a pipe organ for pre-show entertainment.

Though the pipe organ was removed in the 1930's, the other features of the Tivoli are still there. The theatre has gone through several major renovations that began as early as 1976, which have brought it back to its former glory as well as added the modern-day conveniences of fold up arm rests, cup holders, a new sound system, and larger restrooms on the lobby level. The Tivoli screens recent movies — on its only screen! — at bargain prices.

Tweens and Teens Tip: Though parking is no problem, the Tivoli Theatre is located only one block away from the Downers Grove Metra Train Station, which makes this trip "back in time" more of an adventure for those who like to ride the rails. On the weekends and some weeknights, local organists play a Wurlitzer theater organ (installed by the Chicago Area Theatre Organ Enthusiasts) before each show.

Tour/Museum

Unity Temple

875 Lake Street
Oak Park
(708) 383-8873
http://www.unitytemple-utrf.org/index.html
$$
Hours: Mon–Fri 10:30 a.m.–4:30 p.m., Sat 10:00 a.m.–2:00 p.m.,
Sun 1:00 p.m.–4:00 p.m.
Twitter: @unity_temple

In 1905 when lightning struck the steeple of the Unity Church in Oak Park, the wood frame building caught fire and burned to the ground. The day after, Frank Lloyd Wright began to design a new church that would become one of his greatest architectural masterpieces. Wright defied traditional rules and convention for religious architecture and instead created something modern by using poured on-site, exposed concrete. This method was unheard of until then and is now a feature of some of today's greatest buildings. Four years later, the Unity Temple was once again open to its congregation and still stands, more than 100 years later, as a shining example of Wright's revolutionary thinking.

The style, both inside and out, is completely recognizable as Wright's with the abundance of natural light, the blending of the architecture with nature, and the use of art glass and Prairie lighting fixtures. Self-guided tours are available, as are group tours for more than fifteen participants.

Tweens and Teens Tip: Concerts, workshops, films, and other special events are hosted by the Unity Temple Restoration Foundation, which funds the restoration and maintenance of this American treasure. Check the website for an up-to-date schedule.

Xtreme Trampolines

485 Mission Street
Carol Stream, IL 60188
(630) 752-1400
www.xtremetrampolines.com
$$$
Hours: Mon–Thurs 3:00 p.m.–10:00 p.m., Fri 3:00 p.m.–11:00 p.m.,
Sat 10:00 a.m.–11:00 p.m., Sun 11:00 a.m.–9:00 p.m.
Twitter: @x_trampolines

The flying sensation one feels when using a trampoline isn't just for kids anymore. The first trampoline park in the state opened in late 2010 and kids of <u>all</u> ages are welcome to partake in the fun! A mandatory safety video is presented to fun-seekers before the jumping begins on the wall-to-wall trampolines in the 45,000 square foot facility, which also has a large foam pit and a trampoline dodge ball court.

The courts are monitored by facility staff and — so the little ones don't get crushed — divided into three age groups: three to seven, eight to thirteen, and fourteen and older. Pricing is by the hour.

Tweens and Teens Tip: Trampoline Dodge ball has proven to be a huge hit here, and a referee is on duty to make sure everyone plays fair. Trampoline Aerobics classes are offered a few times each week. Visitors should check the website for details.

Southern Suburbs

Also known as the Southland, the southern suburbs are accessed very easily from anywhere else in the area by one of six interstate highways and six rail lines. Toyota Park, home stadium of the Chicago Fire (Major League Soccer) is located in the Southland, as is the First Midwest Bank Amphitheatre, where the biggest names in music come to play. The Southland contains the largest concentration of recreational forest preserves as well as many golf courses, sports facilities, and trails for hiking and biking, which means it's the perfect destination for active families.

Art 4 Soul

18135 Harwood Avenue
Homewood
708-206-1026
www.art4soul.com

Hours: Tues–Fri 10:00 a.m.–6:00 p.m., Sat 10:00 a.m.–5:00 p.m.,
Sun 12:00 p.m.–4:00 p.m.

Artists at heart will find the three floors at Art 4 Soul bursting with creative inspiration. The idea behind Art 4 Soul is unique. It's a combination of an arts and crafts studio with a store full of contemporary and vintage items. Mostly local artists create the items that fill the first level and are for sale. You can find purses, jewelry, home décor items, and much more. The lower level is where you'll find Vintage Soul, which is a resale shop whose inventory changes regularly and capitalizes on the goodness of reusing items that someone else no longer wants or needs. It's a form of recycling, which is great news for those who care about living a greener life.

The upper level of the store is the studio. Here you can paint on a canvas, create a mosaic, design silver clay jewelry, and paint ceramics. Art 4 Soul is an all-inclusive ceramic studio, which means that you only pay for the green ware. When your masterpiece is complete, the folks at Art 4 Soul will fire it and you can return in a week to pick it up.

Tweens and Teens Tip: Art 4 Soul offers general classes on the above-mentioned crafts, and prior to holidays they offer themed sessions as well.

Chicagoland Speedway

500 Speedway Boulevard
Joliet
(815) 727-RACE
www.chicagolandspeedway.com
$$$$$
Hours: Check the website for race times.
Twitter: @chicagolndspdwy

Racing fans rejoice! Chicagoland Speedway is the home of many NASCAR events during the summer, including the NASCAR Sprint Cup Series and the NASCAR Nationwide Series. The speedway is a 1.5-mile D-shaped oval, and the grandstand offers seating for 75,000. The addition of lights for the 2008 season made night racing popular at the speedway, which is located adjacent to the Route 66 Raceway.

Race-goers park for free, and those who wish to camp can get passes to the RV parking area on a first-come, first-served basis. Scanners can be rented in the merchandise midway to add another dimension to this spectator sport.

Tweens and Teens Tip: Only one sealed bottle of water per person is allowed beyond the gates into the grandstand. To save money, bring coolers and leave them in the car. As long as you get a hand-stamp, stadium re-entry is permitted.

CPX Sports

2903 Schweitzer Road
Joliet
815-726-2800 x21
www.cpxsports.com
$$$$$
Hours: Wed–Fri 10:00 a.m.–5:00 p.m., Sat–Sun 9:00 a.m.–6:00 p.m.,
Closed Mon–Tues (Memorial Day–Labor Day),
Sat–Sun 9:00 a.m.–5:00 p.m. (September–May)
Twitter: @cpxsports

Refine your sharpshooting skills with a game of paintball, which is similar in nature to dodge ball. Each player is armed with a marker (gun) and paintballs. The idea of the game is to accomplish a goal such as eliminating others, defending an area or capturing something without getting tagged, or hit, by someone else's paint.

CPX Sports has twenty-four World Class paintball fields that include the Town of Bedlam, Armageddon, Fort Courage, and the Rain Forest. General admission includes all-day CO2 and HP air fills and basic equipment rental. Paintballs (CPX uses field paint only, which is water soluble) cost extra. Players are briefed on safety practices before each game. The minimum age to play at CPX is ten. Check the website for discounted game days.

Tweens and Teens Tip: Anyone under 18 years old must present an Underage Waiver signed by a parent or guardian in order to play. If you get the form notarized by a qualified person at CPX—at no charge—it will be kept on file until the child is 18.

IKEA

750 E. Boughton Road
Bolingbrook
(630) 972-7900
www.ikea.com/us

♦

Hours: Sun 10:00 a.m.–8:00 p.m., Mon–Sat 10:00 a.m.–9:00 p.m.
Twitter: @ikea_chicago

It used to be that the music group "Abba" was the biggest Swedish export in the United States, but all of that has changed. These days, mention Sweden and most people will think "IKEA." These home furnishing product superstores are famous for the low-priced, quality items sold there as much as the customer experience and yes, also for the Swedish meatballs in the café.

The IKEA stores and their innovative assemble-it-yourself products with those goofy Swedish names appeal to shoppers of all ages and budget sizes. Mixed into the brightly colored surroundings are room models that actually show the merchandise displayed together and in use, making it possible to envision how something might look in your own home. The café that serves those famous meatballs in addition to other yummy treats is a tradition you'll want to start with your family, and don't forget to stop in the Food Market for candies, cheeses, and desserts to take home.

Tweens and Teens Tip: IKEA is full of inexpensive home décor items that can spruce up a tween or teen bedroom for less, such as vases, lighting, picture frames, and much more. Check out the "Last Chance" section of the store (just before you reach the check-out area) for slightly-damaged-but-useable and discontinued merchandise for some unbelievable bargains!

Museum

Illinois Aviation Museum
130 S. Clow International Parkway
Bolingbrook
630-771-1937
www.illinoisaviationmuseum.org
✪
Hours: Sat 10:00 a.m.–2:00 p.m. and by appointment

Hangar One at Bolingbrook's Clow International Airport is the home of the collection and programs of the Illinois Aviation Museum, established in 2004. The 6,000 square foot facility is full of restored and replica aircraft, along with current restoration projects that will eventually be displayed.

The historically significant aircraft and artifacts on display at the museum make up a varied and interesting collection. The replica of the Nieuport 12, a plane that served in the Middle East, was originally constructed to perform reconnaissance over the European Western Front. The Lockheed T2 was used in the United States Navy as an all-purpose jet trainer. The Fokker E-3 replica was built from a kit by the museum's WWI Aero Builder's Club and flown for the first time in October 2008. The volunteer staff is more than happy to talk to visitors about these and the other aircraft at the museum.

Tweens and Teens Tip: The Illinois Aviation Museum has great programming for young people. The WWI Aero Builder's Club is open to thirty high school-aged participants. The Experimental Aircraft Association (EAA) Young Eagles program is administered by Clow Airport EAA volunteer pilots and provides flight experience for young people (ages 8–17). Pilots teach Young Eagles about their particular plane and then take them up in the air for a 15–20 minute flight.

Joliet Slammers

1 Mayor Art Schultz Drive
Joliet
(815) 722-2287
www.jolietslammers.com
$$
Hours: Check website for game schedule.
Twitter: @jolietslammers

Silver Cross Field is where you'll find the Joliet Slammers, a member of the Frontier League. Parking near the stadium is free. The Slammers, which replaced the now defunct Joliet Jackhammers, offer fans fun at every turn in addition to some great baseball.

Bowling coupons for participating alleys are up for grabs at the home games. Fans can heckle a designated batter from the opposing team until he strikes out to earn their free game. Other ways for fans to get involved include auditioning (by sending in a CD) to sing the national anthem and to volunteer for the entertainment and games that occur between innings.

Tweens and Teens Tip: Do you have a question for your favorite current Slammers player? Send an email (with the player's name in the subject line) to info@jolietslammers.com, and he will respond!

Sports

Route 66 Raceway
500 Speedway Boulevard
Joliet
(815) 727-RACE
www.route66raceway.com
$$$
Hours: Check the website for race times.
Twitter: @route66raceway

If the terms "Dragster," "Funny Car," and "Christmas Tree" are familiar to you, you're definitely in the right place. The Route 66 Raceway, located adjacent to the Chicagoland Speedway in Joliet, is named in honor of "The Mother Road," Route 66, and includes a .25-mile NHRA-licensed drag strip and .5-mile dirt oval track.

The drag strip hosts a season-long ET Bracket Series for local racers, as well as the Junior Drag Racing League and the NHRA Full Throttle Drag Racing Series. The dirt oval is home to exciting events like obstacle courses, demolition derbies, monster truck competitions and flat track speed racing. The season runs from March through September.

Tweens and Teens Tip: If you're new to drag racing, the website offers a primer that teaches the features of some of the cars as well as what the lights on the Christmas Tree Starting Line System mean!

Sand Ridge Nature Center

15890 Paxton Avenue
South Holland
708-868-0606
http://www.fpdcc.com
✪
Hours: Daily 8:00 a.m.–5:00 p.m.
(March 1–the last Saturday in October),
Daily 8:00 a.m.–4:00 p.m.
(The last Sunday in October–February 28)
Twitter: @FPDCC

Hikers enjoy the four well-marked trails at the Sand Ridge Nature Center because of the different habitats featured. There are prairies, oak savannas and woodlands, marshes, a pond, and ancient sand dunes. The trails range from under a mile to two miles long. While on the trail, you might see gorgeous wildflowers in the spring, a plethora of dragonflies and butterflies in the summer, and beautiful snow drifts in the winter.

Hands-on exhibits and free public nature programs are available year round with the intention to teach visitors about the Calumet region's natural and cultural history. Log cabin reproductions, open to the public, depict the living conditions of 19th century Illinois settlers and are accompanied by pioneer demonstrations on many Wednesday mornings.

Tweens and Teens Tip: Check the event calendar for celebrations on Earth Day, Illinois Archaeology Day, and more. The Settler's Day event is held the Sunday before Thanksgiving and provides visitors with historical re-enactments, hikes, and crafts to make and buy.

Nature

Starved Rock State Park
2668 East 875th Road
Oglesby
815-667-4726
www.starvedrockstatepark.org
✪
Hours: Daily 5:00 a.m.–9:00 p.m.
(Trail parking lots: 8:00 a.m.–sunset)

While it would seem that it is impossible to be completely surrounded by natural elements like waterfalls, cliffs, lush forests, rock formations, and canyons—not to mention eagles and white-tailed deer—anywhere near the Chicago metropolitan area, it is indeed possible and only a short drive away. Starved Rock State Park is a peaceful oasis located less than two hours from Chicago's city center.

The park is a haven for the outdoor enthusiast. Fishing and hunting is allowed with the proper licensing. Hiking and camping are allowed, as are cross-country skiing, ice climbing, boating, horseback riding, and picnicking. Though you can bring the family dog as long as you keep him on a leash (10' or less), rock-climbing, snowmobiling, and cycling is prohibited in the park due to the fragility of the rocks and the trails. If you would like to stay overnight but prefer to be indoors, you can reserve a room or cabin with the Starved Rock Lodge or the Starved Rock Inn.

Tweens and Teens Tip: Stop in at the Visitor's Center when you arrive to get trail maps, souvenirs, snacks and valuable information about the park before you head out to enjoy it. The Visitor's Center is open from 9:00 a.m.–4:00 p.m. daily. If you request it, they will show you a couple of short videos orientating you to the park and its history.

Tri-State Swap-o-Rama
4350 W. 129th Street
Alsip
(708) 344-7300
www.swap-o-rama.com
$
Hours: Sat–Sun 7:00 a.m.–4:00 p.m. (Indoors & Outdoors),
Wed 7:00 a.m.–2:00 p.m. (Outdoors only)

More than seven hundred dealers make the Tri-State Swap-o-Rama a great place to conduct your own treasure hunt. You can find all kinds of new and used items here including furniture and house wares to clothing, crafts, and ceramics. This flea market has a wide variety of vintage items, and the prices are reasonable.

Parking is easy-access and complimentary, and there is a snack bar where you can purchase fast food fare like hot dogs, burgers, nachos, grilled polish sausages, and fries. They even serve breakfast if you're an early bird! Many vendors accept credit cards, but it is suggested (especially for bargaining purposes) that you use cash.

Tweens and Teens Tip: On hot summer days, be prepared for the crowded building to be very warm inside; if you don't enjoy heat it might be a good idea to bargain hunt early in the morning. If you shop toward the end of the day, sellers are more likely to haggle.

Windy City Thunderbolts

14011 S. Kenton Avenue
Crestwood
708-489-2255
www.wcthunderbolts.com
$$
Hours: Check website for game schedule.
Twitter: @wcthunderbolts

Hey, batter batter . . . swing! The Windy City Thunderbolts is an independent baseball team and member of the Frontier League's East Division (not affiliated with the majors in any way). The 2007 and 2008 Frontier League champions play at Standard Bank Stadium to crowds of up to 3,200 spectators. Their season consists of 48 home games and 48 away games.

Game tickets can be purchased individually, by the season, or in Flex Plans (8, 12, or 20 game vouchers per plan). The team also offers a wide variety of group plans, starting with a minimum group size of ten people. Find another family (or two) to tag along and you'll be eligible to take advantage of the "Field of Dreams" package, which includes admission, a hot dog, chips, ice cream, and soda for each person, and your group can be on the field for the National Anthem, too!

Tweens and Teens Tip: Look for the Thunderbolts' special "Campin' Out" event, where families can enjoy an evening game and then camp overnight in the outfield!

Over the Borders

Though heading over the border into Indiana or Wisconsin definitely means you've left Chicagoland, there is some major Fun to be had in less than a couple hours' drive—with the exception of the Water Park at Blue Harbor Resort in Sheboygan, Wisconsin. You'll have to drive about three hours to get there, but it's worth it!

Bristol Renaissance Faire

12550-120th Avenue
Kenosha, WI
(847) 395-7773
www.renfair.com/Bristol/
$$$$
Hours: 10:00 a.m.–7:00 p.m. Sat–Sun throughout the summer only,
plus Labor Day Monday
Twitter: @bristolrenfaire

If you're looking for *olde*-style fun, as well as a re-creation of a day when Queen Elizabeth visited Bristol, England in the 1500's, the 30-acre grounds of the Bristol Renaissance Faire is the place. A 16th century immersion experience begins immediately upon entry to the Faire, where lords, ladies, jesters, and others — in full period costume — regale the crowds with their stories and antics. There is jousting, swordplay, dancing, juggling, and comedy around every corner, and the interactive nature of this event is a memorable one for families.

Rides and games are available for an extra charge, as is a plethora of food choices (including the humongous turkey drumsticks you would expect) that goes above and beyond what is usually offered at an outdoor festival. Merchants of handmade treasures dot the faire; look for blown glass, costumes, metalwork, toys, leather goods, soaps, and more. In addition to products, services such as hair braiding, henna painting, handwriting analysis, and tarot readings are easily found.

Tweens and Teens Tip: Check out "RenQuest," the Faire's live action fantasy-play. Create your character online (at the Bristol RenQuest Facebook Fan Page) before you arrive at the Faire, and look for the secret of the dragon's egg while you're exploring the grounds.

Food

Franks Diner

508-58th Street
Kenosha, WI
(262) 657-1017
www.franksdinerkenosha.com

Hours: Mon–Fri 6:00 a.m.–2:00 p.m. Sat 7:00 a.m.–2:00 p.m.,
Sun 7:00 a.m.–1:00 p.m.

An old railway dining car was transported on a railroad flat car to Kenosha from its origin in New Jersey and pulled to its current location by six horses all the way back in 1926. The original owner, Anthony Franks, added a dining room in 1935 and then a larger kitchen in the mid-1940s. The Franks family operated the diner until 2001 when the current owners, regular diner patrons themselves, purchased it. Since then, many renovations have been made and Franks Diner has even been featured on Guy Fieri's Food Network show, "Diners, Drive-Ins, and Dives," bringing a whole new wave of regular customers to the little diner that could.

Perhaps the most famous dish coming out of the kitchen area is the Garbage Plate, a breakfast dish that is so huge they offer a half plate option. The menu includes a full range of breakfast and lunch options, which are served up with style and sass (their motto is "Order what you want; eat what you get"!), all in all a winning recipe for this staple of downtown Kenosha.

Tweens and Teens Tip: Between the small size of the restaurant and the quality of food served there, Franks Diner is very often crowded. Go early to have the best chance of a shorter wait (but don't be surprised if many others beat you to it), and remember that no orders are taken 30 minutes before closing, which is when the staff locks the doors!

Garwood Orchards and Farm Market

5911 West 50 South
La Porte, IN
(219) 362-4385
www.garwoodorchard.com

♦

Hours: Market is open daily, 8:30 a.m.–6:00 p.m. (U-Pick Farm is open 8:30 a.m.–5:00 p.m. seasonally from June through October.)
Twitter: @garwoodorchard

The Garwood family knows that a sixth-generation family owned and operated farm is a rare thing, and they are extremely involved in their business in order to ensure its survival for future generations. The u-pick aspect of the business includes a selection of vegetables (peppers, tomatoes, eggplant, green beans) and fruits (apples, berries, pumpkin) that is more diverse than other area u-pick farms.

It is advisable to check the website ahead of your visit for picking availability. When you arrive, you'll get empty picking containers at the front of the farm and then board a wagon that will deliver you to the proper picking area. If you would rather purchase ready-picked fruits and vegetables, the farm's market can easily accommodate. Also sold here are homemade products such as apple butter, sauces, and jellies, as well as burgers and bratwursts.

Tweens and Teens Tip: Check out Applefest, an area tradition for families that is held annually in the fall. Enjoy live music, u-pick apples and pumpkins, and an arts and crafts fair.

Indiana Dunes State Park
1600 North 25 E
Chesterton, IN
(219) 926-1952
www.in.gov/dnr/parklake/2980.htm
$$
Hours: Daily 7:00 a.m.–11:00 p.m.
Twitter: @indianadunes

The fifteen-mile stretch of Indiana Dunes National Lakeshore, which runs from Portage to Michigan City, is a popular getaway spot for Chicagoland residents. Situated in the middle is Indiana Dunes State Park, which is a three-mile stretch of beaches made of soft, fine sand and beautiful landscape.

Visitors can enjoy swimming and sunning, as well as smelt fishing and picnicking. The Indiana Dunes State Park Nature Center educates visitors on the formation of the dunes as well as the plants and animals found there. Ask the staff for advice on the hiking trails in the area, which vary in length, level of difficulty, and scenery.

Tweens and Teens Tip: Look for the Chicago skyline on a clear day to get a unique perspective on the city, and listen for the singing sands, a natural phenomenon caused by the wind passing over the dunes and found in very few places around the world.

Jelly Belly Warehouse Tour

10100 Jelly Belly Lane
Pleasant Prairie, WI
(866) TOUR-JBC
www.jellybelly.com/visit_jelly_belly/index.aspx
✪
Hours: Daily 9:00 a.m.–4:00 p.m.

This informative, 30-minute tour consists of a train ride on the "Jelly Belly Express" through the warehouse and makes several stops during which passengers can take a look at the Jelly Belly-making process from start to finish (as well as other candy products produced by the company), with the help of video presentations.

The facility has a full retail store where you can purchase the latest in apparel emblazoned with the company logo as well as, of course, a large variety of candy and other novelty items. The sample bar is quite popular. Here you can taste—for free—more than 100 varieties of Jelly Bellys, gummies, chocolates, and other treats.

Tweens and Teens Tip: The retail store also sells factory seconds; availability changes from day-to-day. Look for value-sized bags of "Belly Flops," which are Jelly Bellys that are cosmetically inferior to first-quality beans but taste just as delicious.

Prime Outlets at Pleasant Prairie

11211 120th Avenue (I-94 & Hwy. 165)
Pleasant Prairie, WI
(262) 857-2101
www.primeoutlets.com

♦

Hours: Mon–Sat 10:00 a.m.–9:00 p.m., Sun 10:00 a.m.–7:00 p.m.
Twitter: @primeoutlets

Also see Prime Outlets at Huntley, Northwestern Suburbs.

Tour

Sprecher Brewery

701 W. Glendale Avenue
Glendale, WI
(414) 964-BREW
www.sprecherbrewery.com
$
Hours: Tour start times vary; check website for details.
Twitter: @sprecherbrewery

Touring a microbrewery is a great way to get up close and personal with a company that emphasizes quality in its handcrafted products. Products manufactured at the Sprecher Brewery—which was founded in 1985—have steadily gained momentum and are now sold in stores all over the Midwest, as well as in Florida and New York.

The family-friendly tour begins and ends in the gift shop, which is full of Sprecher memorabilia, apparel, glassware, foods, and of course, gourmet sodas and beers. Visitors walk through the aging cellar, bottling line and warehouse as they learn how Sprecher beers are produced. The penultimate stop on the tour is a Munich-style indoor beer garden where adults 21 and older can try up to four samples of beer (each person chooses from ten varieties on tap) in a tasting glass, which is theirs to keep. Kids (and adults) get unlimited samples of all seven Sprecher gourmet sodas.

Tweens and Teens Tip: Because tour sizes are limited, reservations are required. Before you leave, stock up on Sprecher beverages, because the prices at the brewery are much cheaper than in your local grocery store. Look for overruns on the private label cherry soda that Sprecher makes for Cherry Republic in Michigan called "Boom Chugga Lugga." If you see it there, grab it while you can, because it moves quickly!

Thompson's Strawberry Farm
14000-75th Street
Bristol, WI
(262) 857-2353
www.thompsonstrawberryfarm.com
♦

Hours: Open mid-June through mid-July for strawberries,
September for raspberries, and October for pumpkins;
check website or call for operating hours.

It's not easy to find "pick-your-own-fruit" farms in the Chicago area, though there are a few for those who prefer to bring their own produce directly from the field to the table. Thompson's is located west of Kenosha, Wisconsin (and just north of Antioch, Illinois) and provides fruity fun from summer to fall.

Because Mother Nature does not work on a reliable schedule, it's imperative that you check the website or make a phone call to the farm ahead of time to make sure that there are enough ripe berries available for picking. Upon your arrival, the staff will point out where to pick your fruit and then you're on your own, free to pick as many basketfuls as you like. When you drive to the farm exit, staff members will count your baskets and payment is made at that time, in cash or check only.

Tweens and Teens Tip: Go green and save money by bringing baskets from previous visits, because you'll save 25 cents on each when you refill them with berries. Young people who have an interest in the culinary arts should check the website for recipes that the whole family can make, extending the enjoyment of strawberry season well into winter.

Lodging/Water Fun

The Water Park at Blue Harbor Resort

725 Blue Harbor Drive
Sheboygan, WI
(920) 452-2900
www.blueharborresort.com
$$$
Hours: Daily 9:00 a.m.–9:00 p.m.

Although Blue Harbor is a fabulous family destination for overnight stays, you don't have to be a guest in order to spend the day there, getting wet. The S.S. Minnow area, which features a 79,000-gallon recreation pool, a lazy river, and a whirlpool is fun for all ages. The park includes seven waterslides, the largest of which are the Soaker and the Splashdown. Each is three stories high and exits and re-enters the building along the way before depositing riders in the pool at the bottom. Breaker Bay Pier is a four-story water activity hub, full of sprinklers, tubes, and other interactive features. It is topped off by a tipping ship, which dumps 1000 gallons of water onto the play area below every few minutes.

The resort also has an outdoor pool called Flapper's Landing, which is open only during the summer months. A patio area with tables and chairs is adjacent to the pool, and guests can sit and admire Lake Michigan while soaking up the sun.

Tweens and Teens Tip: Because the guests of the resort get priority use of the water parks, it is highly recommended that non-guests call on the day of their desired visit to make sure that space is available. If you don't want to leave it to chance, check the website often for current specials on overnight stays. Water park admissions are included in the room rate.

Major Sports in Chicagoland

Chicago sports fans can be described using many colorful adjectives, but if they had to be summarized with only one word it would probably be "loyal." The trials and tribulations of many of the teams have tested the adoring public to their very limits, but in the end these fans are forever.

The Chicago sports spectator experience — once you're at the stadium, arena, rink, field, or ballpark — is, obviously, unique to each team. What most of them have in common are higher-end ticket prices, traffic headaches, and expensive parking, concessions, and souvenirs. Don't let all of that deter you, because it's worth it. This is Chicago, after all. It is home to some of the greatest sport franchises in the world.

Here is a list of major sports teams in Chicagoland, along with the most basic information you need in order to begin your game planning strategy. Information listed includes where they play when at home, the phone number for tickets, the web address, Twitter handle, and the league to which they belong. The team websites contain the most up-to-date information, including schedules, team news and events, and current ticket pricing.

Chicago Bears

Soldier Field
1410 Museum Campus Drive
Chicago
(312) 235-7000
www.chicagobears.com
Twitter: @chicagobearscom
National Football League

Chicago Blackhawks

United Center
1901 W. Madison Street
Chicago
(312) 455-4000
www.blackhawks.nhl.com
Twitter: @nhlblackhawks
National Hockey League

Chicago Bulls

United Center
1901 W. Madison Street
Chicago
(312) 455-4000
www.nba.com/bulls
Twitter: @chicagobulls
National Basketball Association

Chicago Cubs

Wrigley Field
1060 West Addison Street
Chicago
(773) 404-CUBS

www.cubs.com
Twitter: @cubs
Major League Baseball (National)

Chicago Fire

Toyota Park
7000 S. Harlem Avenue
Bridgeview
(708) 594-7200
www.chicago-fire.com
Twitter: @chicagofire
Major League Soccer

Chicago Red Stars

(At press time, operations were temporarily suspended.
Check website for details.)
Toyota Park
7000 S. Harlem Avenue
Bridgeview
1-866-WPS-2009
www.womensprosoccer.com/chicago
Twitter: @chicagoredstars
Women's Professional Soccer League

Chicago Sky

Allstate Arena
6920 Mannheim Road
Rosemont
(866) SKY-WNBA
www.chicagosky.net
Twitter: @wnbachicagosky
Women's National Basketball Association

Chicago Slaughter
Sears Centre Arena
533 Prairie Stone Parkway
Hoffman Estates
847-310-3190
http://chicago-slaughter.com
Twitter: @chislaughter
Indoor Football League

Chicago White Sox
U.S. Cellular Field
333 W. 35th Street
Chicago
(866) SOX-GAME
www.whitesox.com
Twitter: @whitesox
Major League Baseball (American)

Chicago Wolves
Allstate Arena
6920 N. Mannheim Road
Rosemont
(847) 635-6601
www.chicagowolves.com
Twitter: @chicago_wolves
American Hockey League

Touring Chicagoland

Sometimes it's more about the journey than the destination. Many companies in the Chicago area offer tours that provide visitors great information about the city from different perspectives. Tours that concentrate on the skyline, the neighborhoods, the architecture, the food, or the history are in abundance in this town, and they don't all take place on a bus. Whether you like to travel by foot, on wheels, across water, by horse, or on a Segway, you can find the perfect tour on which to soak in the city.

Make sure to check out your options on the web. These companies offer numerous tours (many of which are company-exclusives) of varying lengths, at all times of day and evening. Know where the tours begin and end, as many companies have several starting points. The FAQ sections online will have information about for whom their tours are recommended, as well as restrictions and permissions when it comes to bringing food, drink, and even the family dog along.

The following list includes the name of each touring company, starting locations, phone number, website, modes of transport, and a short summary of its offerings:

Antique Coach and Carriage
Michigan Avenue & Huron Street
Chicago
(773) 735-9400
www.antiquecoach-carriage.com/tours.html
Horse Carriages

Ride around the city in an open or closed carriage. Drivers have pre-planned routes to choose from, or you can choose your own route.

Bobby's Bike Hike Chicago
465 N. McClurg Court
Chicago
(312) 915-0995
www.bobbysbikehike.com
Twitter: @bobbysbikehike
Bicycles

Ride a comfortable cruiser (or bring your own wheels to get a tour discount) on the *Lakefront Neighborhoods Tour*, the *City Lights at Night Tour*, or the *Obama Bike Tour*, which begins in the President's Hyde Park neighborhood.

Chicago Elevated
Various Starting Points
Chicago
(773) 593-4873
www.chicagoelevated.com
Twitter: @chicagoelevated
On Foot

Stay warm and dry as you take an entertaining 60- or 90-minute architecture tour on the city's enclosed underground—and occasionally elevated—walkway, one of Chicago's best-kept secrets. Loop and Riverwalk tours are also available.

Chicago Film Tour
Clark Street between Ontario & Ohio Streets, next to the
Rock N Roll McDonald's
Chicago
(312) 593-4455
www.chicagofilmtour.com
Twitter: @chifilm
Buses

Tour sites where over fifty movies were shot. Movies include "Ferris Bueller's Day Off," "The Blues Brothers," and "The Dark Knight." Passengers watch movie scenes at each location.

Chicago Food Planet Tours
Various Starting Points
Chicago
(212) 209-3370
www.chicagofoodplanet.com
Twitter: @ChiFoodPlanet
On Foot

Taste the best of what Chicago neighborhoods have to offer on these three-hour walking tours.

Chicago Greeter Free Tours
Various Starting Points
Chicago
(312) 744-8000
www.chicagogreeter.com
On Foot, Public Transportation

Local enthusiasts volunteer for this Chicago Office of Tourism program. Tour possibilities are endless: experience neighborhoods, parks, museums, shops and boutiques, restaurants, the lakefront, or an area of your own suggestion.

Chicago Hauntings Tours
600 N. Clark Street
Chicago
(888) 446-7891
www.chicagohauntings.com
Buses

Learn the history behind various city locations that are known for paranormal activity. Tours are given only at night.

Chicago History Museum Tour
(by Chicago Line Cruises)
465 N. McClurg Court
Chicago
(312) 527-1977
www.chicagoline.com
Boats

These architecture and historical cruises educate passengers about how Chicago came into existence and grew into one of the world's great cities.

Chicago Horse & Carriage Ltd.
Michigan Avenue & Pearson Street
Chicago
(312) 988-9090
www.chicagocarriage.com
Horse Carriages

Popular tour destinations include Michigan Avenue, State Street, Millennium Park, Lincoln Park, Buckingham Fountain, and more. Rides are 30 minutes to two hours long, depending on the area you choose, and open and closed carriages are available.

Chicago Neighborhood Tours

Various Starting Points
Chicago
(312) 742-1190
www.chicagoneighborhoodtours.com
On Foot

Experience the culture and people of Chicago neighborhoods on four and a half hour walking tours that include light refreshments. Specialty tours of Chicago churches, Greek, Irish, and Polish neighborhoods, and more are also available.

Chicago Photo Safaris

Various Starting Points
Chicago
(312) 789-5645
www.chicagophotosafaris.com
Twitter: @chicagophotosaf
On Foot

Those who have a serious interest in photography—no matter the skill level—will learn how (and where) to create fabulous pictures in one of the most beautiful cities in the world. Pre-safari advice on what equipment to bring and post-safari photo critiques are available.

Chicago Pizza Tours

Wells Street & Ontario Street
Chicago
(630) 842-0372
www.chicagopizzatours.com
Twitter: @chipizzatour
Buses

Taste a slice from four Chicago pizzerias that have their own twist on creating a great pie. Experience Neapolitan, stuffed, and thin crust versions. Tours are two hours long.

Chicago Red Cap Walking Tours
Chicago River at Michigan Avenue
Chicago
(312) 927-0689
www.chicagoredcaptours.com
On Foot

The details of Chicago's colorful history and beautiful architecture are shared with participants during a two-hour walking tour. Tours begin at the statue of Jean Baptiste Point du Sable, located on the east side of Michigan Avenue, north of the Chicago River.

City Segway Tours
400 East Randolph Street
Chicago
(312) 819-0186
www.citysegwaytours.com/chicago
Twitter: @citysegwaytours
Segways

After a 30-minute Segway orientation session, tour the city on this unique single-person mode of transport. Tours are three hours long.

Mercury Skyline Cruiseline
112 E. Wacker Drive
Chicago
(312) 332-1366
www.mercuryskylinecruiseline.com
Boats

Mercury Skyline's educational (and lively) river tours focusing on the history of bridges, skyscrapers, and other landmarks are a beautiful and fun way to enjoy the city. Night cruises and canine cruises are also offered.

Mystic Blue Cruises
Navy Pier
Chicago
(877) 299-7783
www.mysticbluecruises.com
Twitter: @entertaincruise
Boats

Enjoy a buffet brunch, lunch, or dinner (and dancing) as you sail South along the lake shore, past the Adler Planetarium, North to Montrose Harbor, and then South again, returning to Navy Pier.

Odyssey Cruises
Navy Pier
Chicago
(866) 305-2469
www.odysseycruises.com/chicago
Twitter: @entertaincruise
Boats

Dining, dancing, and live entertainment are a big part of these cruises on the lake. Don't forget to gaze at the city skyline from a rare perspective.

Seadog Cruises
Navy Pier
Chicago
(888) 636-7737
www.seadogcruises.com
Speedboats

If you love to go fast, take a speedboat tour of the city's architecture and of the lake, or an extreme thrill ride tour that travels 30% faster than the other boats in their fleet.

Shoreline Sightseeing
Navy Pier
Chicago
(312) 222-9328
www.shorelinesightseeing.com
Twitter: @shorelinetours
Boats, Water Taxis

Shoreline offers skyline, fireworks, and architecture cruises, featuring the history of more than forty of Chicago's distinctive landmarks. They also offer water taxi service between Navy Pier, Museum Campus, Michigan Avenue, Wells Street & Wacker Drive, and Union Station.

Spirit of Chicago
Navy Pier
Chicago
(866) 273-2469
www.spiritofchicago.com
Twitter: @entertaincruise
Boats

Glide along Lake Michigan past famous landmarks like Soldier Field, Buckingham Fountain, and the AON Center while dining and dancing. Cruises are available during the day or night.

Untouchable Tours
600 N. Clark Street
Chicago
(773) 881-1195
www.gangstertour.com
Buses

Chicago's Original Gangster Tour takes participants to infamous locations like the St. Valentine's Day Massacre site, the Biograph Theatre, and Capone rival Dion O'Banion's flower shop.

Wendella Sightseeing

400 North Michigan Avenue
Chicago
(312) 337-1446
www.wendellaboats.com
Twitter: @wendellaboats
Boats, Water Taxis

Family owned and operated since 1935, Wendella offers *Chicago River Architecture* tours and combined *Lake and River* tours. Water taxi service between Michigan Avenue, LaSalle/Clark Streets, Madison Street, and Chinatown is also available.

Look for detailed information about these city tours, elsewhere in the book:

Hot Dogs and Pizza in Chicagoland

Chicago is home to thousands of wonderful eateries in every flavor, ethnicity, ambiance, and price range, so many that it would truly be impossible to try them all. Some of the great chefs of the world (Charlie Trotter, Homaro Cantu, Rick Bayless, Tony Mantuano, Gale Gand, Rick Tramonto, and many more) create unforgettable dining experiences right here in their own Chicago restaurants. Fine dining is only part of the equation when it comes to the food for which Chicago is known. Ask any tourist what they'd like to eat most, and they'll likely respond with "hot dogs" or "pizza," and quite possibly, both!

Take heed! Regarding hot dogs, it's important to note that not only does a proper Chicago-style hot dog *not* have ketchup on it, but also, many restaurants won't put it on for you, even if you request it. A real Chicago hot dog is made with the following ingredients: all-beef dog, yellow mustard, sweet relish, chopped onions, tomato wedges, a pickle spear, sport peppers, celery salt, and a poppy seed bun.

By the way, did you know that Chicago is famous for deep-dish AND stuffed pizza? Deep-dish is just like it sounds: a single, thick crust pizza cooked in a deep pan, with higher edges. Stuffed pizza has a double crust with ingredients inside. Of course, other types of pizza joints can be found in Chicago too (like Chicago Pizza and Oven Grinder, profiled on page 52).

This partial list of places where you can get the perfect Chicago dog or the heartiest pizza will give you more than enough to choose from when stomachs start to growl! Check out their websites for city and suburban location listings, phone numbers, and menus.

Chicago Dogs

Hot Doug's

Famous for: Serving many different types of sausage, hence the self-proclaimed "Sausage Superstore and Encased Meat Emporium" title.
City Location: Avondale
www.hotdougs.com
Twitter: @hotdougs

Poochie's

Famous for: Char dogs and fresh-cut fries
Suburban Location: Skokie
www.poochieshotdogs.com

Portillo's Hot Dogs

Famous for: Being the largest Chicago dog chain in the area, great tasting hot dogs
City Locations: W. Ontario
Suburban Locations: Addison, Arlington Heights, Batavia, Bloomingdale, Bolingbrook, Crestwood, Crystal Lake, Downers Grove, Elk Grove Village, Elmhurst, Forest Park, Glendale Heights, Naperville, Niles, Northlake, Oak Lawn, Oswego, Rolling Meadows, Schaumburg, Shorewood, Skokie, St. Charles, Streamwood, Summit, Sycamore, Tinley Park, Vernon Hills, Villa Park, Willowbrook
www.portillos.com

Superdawg (profiled on page 74)

Famous for: 1950s kitsch, Carhop service
City Location: Norwood Park
Suburban Location: Wheeling
Airport Location: Chicago Midway International Airport
www.superdawg.com

Twitter: @superdawg & @superdawgwheel

Wiener's Circle
Famous for: Char dogs and cheese fries, plus a verbally abusive staff and non-family-friendly late-night atmosphere
City Location: Lincoln Park
No official website; fan site is at www.wienerscircle.net

Chicago Pizza

Art of Pizza
Famous for: Deep-dish pizza
City Location: Lakeview
No website. (773) 327-5600
Twitter: @artofpizza

Bacino's/Bella Bacino's
Famous for: Stuffed pizza
City Locations: Lincoln Park, Loop
Suburban Locations: La Grange
www.bacinos.com
Twitter: @bacinoschicago

Edwardo's Natural Pizza
Famous for: Stuffed pizza
City Locations: Hyde Park, Halsted, North Dearborn, Printer's Row
Suburban Locations: Oak Park, Skokie, Wheeling
www.edwardos.com
Twitter: @edwardospizza

Gino's East
Famous for: Deep-dish pizza
City Locations: Loop, O'Hare Plaza, Lakeview
Suburban Locations: Deerfield, Lake Zurich, Libertyville,
Naperville, Rolling Meadows, St. Charles, Wheaton
www.ginoseast.com
Twitter: @ginoseast

Giordano's
Famous for: Stuffed pizza
City Locations: Belmont, Jackson, Pulaski, Rush Street, Hyde
Park, Montrose, Logan Square, Greek Town, Midway, Sheridan,
Irving Park, Prudential Plaza
Suburban Locations: Addison, Algonquin, Buffalo Grove,
Downers Grove, Evanston, Fox Lake, Glen Ellyn, Gurnee,
Joliet, Lake Zurich, Morton Grove, Naperville, North Aurora,
Oak Brook Terrace, Oak Park, Orland Park, Oswego, Plainfield,
Rosemont, Streamwood, Sycamore, Westchester, Willowbrook
www.giordanos.com
Twitter: @giordanospizza

Lou Malnati's
Famous for: Deep-dish pizza
City Locations: Bucktown/Wicker Park, Lawndale, Lincoln
Park, River North, South Loop
Suburban Locations: Bloomingdale, Buffalo Grove, Carol
Stream/Wheaton, Elk Grove Village, Elmhurst, Evanston,
Geneva, Grayslake, Highland Park, Lake Forest, Lake Zurich,
Lakewood, Libertyville, Lincolnwood, Mount Prospect,
Naperville, Northbrook, Palatine, Park Ridge, Schaumburg,
Western Springs, Wilmette
www.loumalnatis.com
Twitter: @loumalnatis

Pizano's

Famous for: Deep-dish pizza
City Locations: State Street, The Loop
Suburban Location: Glenview
www.pizanoschicago.com
Twitter: @pizanoschicago

Pizzeria Uno/Pizzeria Due

Famous for: Deep-dish pizza
City Locations: Wabash Avenue, East Ohio
Suburban Locations: Gurnee, Schaumburg
www.unos.com
Twitter: @unochicagogrill

Crafting in Chicagoland

Some days call for hands-on activity and something you can bring home. In addition to a plethora of great park district programs in the arts and crafts category, the Chicago area has a wealth of "do-it-yourself" craft shops with open studio time and classes to satisfy the most creative of families. The rewards of making something with your own hands while accompanied by those you love can far outlast the couple of hours spent actually creating it.

Check out this partial list of homemade fun zones, and be sure to call ahead to check on business hours and pricing before you get in the car!

Archiver's
What it is: Scrapbooking and paper crafts
Suburban Locations: Algonquin, Downers Grove, Gurnee, Naperville, Niles, Orland Park
www.archiversonline.com
Twitter: @archivers

Art 4 Soul (profiled on page 164)
What it is: jewelry making, paint your own pottery, mosaics, painting
Suburban Location: Homewood
www.art4soul.com
Twitter: @art4soul

Beadniks

What it is: Beading, jewelry making
City Location: Wicker Park
www.beadniks.com/chicago
Twitter: @beadnikschi

Caravan Beads

What it is: Beading, jewelry making
City Location: Lakeview
www.caravanchicago.com
Twitter: @caravanchicago

Clay Monet

What it is: Paint your own pottery
Suburban Location: Lake Zurich
www.claymonet.com

Color Me Mine

What it is: Paint your own pottery
Suburban Locations: Burr Ridge, Crystal Lake, Geneva,
Glenview, Kildeer, Naperville
www.colormemine.com
Twitter: @colormemineent

Craft Fancy

What it is: Scrapbooking and paper crafting
Suburban Location: Arlington Heights
www.craftfancy.com
Twitter: @craftfancy

FiredWorks

What it is: Paint your own pottery
Suburban Location: Highland Park
www.hpfiredworks.com

Glazed Expressions

What it is: Paint your own pottery
City Location: Lincoln Park
Suburban Locations: Downers Grove, Wilmette
www.myglazedexpressions.com

Lillstreet Art Center

What it is: Classes and workshops in ceramics, jewelry, painting, drawing, printmaking, textiles, and glass
City Location: Lakeview
www.lillstreet.com
Twitter: @lillstreet

Out on a Whim

What it is: Paint your own pottery
Suburban Location: Glen Ellyn
www.outonawhim.info

Pottery Bayou (profiled on page 157)

What it is: Paint your own pottery
Suburban Location: Naperville
www.pottery-bayou.com

Sister Arts Studio

What it is: Creative Classes in knitting, weaving, felting, crochet, and jewelry design
City Location: Lincoln Park
www.sisterartsstudio.com
Twitter: @sisterarts

The Place To Bead (profiled on page 156)

What it is: Beading, jewelry making
Suburban Location: Naperville
www.theplacetobead.com

Windy City Scrapbooking

What it is: Scrapbooking and paper crafts
City Location: DePaul
www.windycityscrapbooking.com
Twitter: @windycityscrap

Part Three
The Extras

Creating a Personalized Family Summer Camp

What to do, what to do? The activities in this book can be enjoyed as individual field trips, but combining a few attractions into a daylong itinerary adds a little more adventure into the mix. You can even go above and beyond by planning a personalized Summer Camp, which will keep your family busy, provide many opportunities to learn and bond, and—most importantly—create lifelong memories for everyone involved.

Traditional summer camp can often be cost-prohibitive for a one-career family, but it's great for parents who both work because their children are having all sorts of fun during school vacation, while being supervised at the same time by an outside provider. Do-it-yourself camp is a great option for families who either have one parent at home or can't justify the expense of camp as it relates to working a full schedule during the summer months. All it requires is some advance planning and good organizational skills. For best results, your Family Camp should be designed as if you were offering it to outsiders. It's important to set and stick to certain guidelines; that way, you will be committing to hold Family Camp up high on the priority list, and your kids will realize that this is different from any other summer full of generic play dates that are scheduled and canceled on a whim.

Noting Individual Preferences

The first step in planning your own Family Camp is to give your tweens and teens a chance to flip through the activities in this book, and ask them to make some personal notes. Gather everyone together and talk about what each person wants to do. Make some notes of your own, preferably in some sort of notebook that you will continue to use during the summer. Then, ask yourself some questions:

- Did certain activities seem popular among your family members, appearing on the list of more than one child?
- Did they only choose destinations your family has previously visited?
- Did they only choose destinations that you've never experienced?
- How close to (or far from) your home are the selected activities?
- Does the family list include activities that run the gamut as far as costs are concerned?

Besides thinking about the answers to these questions and discussing adjustments to the master list, you'll need to research online (the kids can help!) to get current admission pricing by the numbers. Write down the fee totals in your notebook. All of these factors (and more, as they come up during the process) will help you make the best decisions about where your family will go. Keep your notes handy, because you'll need them later.

Setting a Budget

After you've tossed some ideas around as a family, it's time to set and discuss the budget. Depending upon whether you're planning Family Camp for the entire summer or just for a week or two, you can divide the total budget into manageable (weekly or monthly) chunks. Explain what the budget will cover to your tweens and teens. For example, will the camp budget cover the cost of transportation, admissions, meals, *and* souvenirs, or just one or two of those expenses? Everyone should know in advance if they will have to create individual budgets to take care of certain costs.

One way to teach great lessons about money all summer long is to make the camp budget inclusive of all expenses except for personal souvenirs. By doing so, the kids will learn about setting aside part of their allowances according to the camp agenda and whether there is the potential for souvenir purchases. They'll also think twice—or three times—before spending their own cash on useless junk that will end up at the bottom of a closet. Keep in mind (and stress to everyone) that a summer's worth of memories and the photographs that will come with them are really the best—and cheapest—souvenirs. Once you communicate that idea effectively, you may just find that by summer's end you'll have kids who have saved lots of their own money and truly focused on the family time, instead of the stuff they brought home.

Making a Calendar

Once the budget amount is set, it's time to plan where you're going, and when you're going there. Obtain a blank calendar that you can use especially for Family Camp (buy one at the store, print one from the internet, or create one using a computer program like Microsoft Publisher or Apple's iCal). Before you get into the planning of Family Camp activities, be sure to jot down doctor and dentist appointments and other obligations that take precedence over camp. If you are working part-time during the summer or need to be away for other reasons, mark those dates and times on the calendar too, because it'll save a few headaches later.

Grab your notes, a pencil, and the calendar, and coordinate another family meeting for date planning purposes. Keep the following in mind:

- Remember to figure costs for each activity *per family*! It's helpful to write down the estimated costs on each scheduled calendar day; when you see it in black and white, shuffling the schedule around becomes easier.
- Learn whether attractions have free- or reduced-admission days and take advantage of them whenever possible.

- Try to schedule a variety of activities (for example, don't visit only museums for days at a time) to keep things fresh.

- Mix up the activities according to each child's interests so that someone is not walking around completely bored for extended periods (remember this variation on a famous quote by Abraham Lincoln: *"You can please all the people some of the time, and some of the people all the time, but you cannot please all the people all the time."*)

- If you will be covering more than one place in a day, plan itineraries in such a way that makes sense time-wise and gasoline-wise, because you don't want to waste either one.

- Consider the weather, specifically the summer heat. A river cruise might be better in the morning before the sun is at its hottest and water parks are most enjoyable in the afternoon.

It's an important part of the learning process (and family/team dynamic) to realize that flexibility is the key. For example, if the family has decided to spend more money during one week in order to see a professional sports game, it will be necessary to choose less expensive activities for the rest of that period—or for the next week—in order to stay on or under budget. This part of camp planning can be an invaluable lesson on finances in action, one that can actually help set the foundation in your children's own spending habits later on. It's important to involve them as much as possible while realizing that they will be watching your decisions carefully throughout the process.

Contingency Plans

Any good camp program has built-in contingency plans. Though you will stress that "if it's on the calendar, we're doing it," you still need to plan as much as possible for unexpected situations.

Rain is an inevitable event during the summer, no matter where you live. Be prepared to substitute one activity for another if Mother

Nature refuses to cooperate. Movie theaters are great places to enjoy on rainy days, as are museums. Should it rain on your parade (or Segway tour, or Arboretum visit), find something else during that week that you can switch it with. If you substitute the original plan with something that wasn't on the calendar initially, decide as a family if the budget can withstand rescheduling it without cutting back on something else.

In the event that one of your tweens or teens is unable to participate in camp on any given day, it's a great idea to take whoever is left to a destination that held no interest whatsoever for the absent child. Having organized notes on secondary activities will help you roll with the punches.

Special Projects

Depending on the ages and interests of your children, your Family Camp can include added creative elements that will enhance the summer. Of course, these ideas are only the tip of the iceberg. If your family is particularly inspired, you can brainstorm this category, too. Many of these activities are great for rainy days! Special projects include (but aren't limited to!):

- *Camp apparel:* t-shirts, hats, and tote bags can be custom-ordered or—better yet—homemade as a part of a camp activity.

- *Postcard bundles:* collect postcards from each activity, when available. Stack them, punch a hole in the corner, and thread a ribbon or metal ring through them to create an inexpensive and space-saving keepsake of the summer.

- *Scrapbooks:* Collect photos, ticket stubs, and other memorabilia to create a permanent record of each year's Family Camp.

- *Pen pals:* Agree to exchange accounts of your adventures with out-of-state friends or family members who also have tweens and teens. This can be done on postcards, on stationery, or via e-mail.

- *Holiday gifts:* Plan some crafting days with the holidays in mind. Most people love to receive homemade gifts, and your kids will love giving them!

Creating a well-rounded itinerary for Family Camp is easy when you work together, and it can provide memories for years to come. Marking your agenda down on paper will show your tweens and teens that you are committed to the plans, and more importantly will show that you are committed to spending time *with them.* A summer full of new, fun, and even educational experiences is a great way to bond as a family unit, and will mean as much to your kids as it will to you.

Chicagoland History

Ahh, Chicago. City of big shoulders, Second City, the Windy City . . . no matter the name, the metropolis of the Midwest has been through many major changes since its discovery in the 1600s. The city has blossomed especially nicely over the past one hundred years, after quite literally rising from the ashes. Having a reputation that combines mismatched components such as gangsters, harsh winters, beautiful architecture, political corruption, deep-dish pizza, infamous sports teams, and the home base of the 44th President of the United States is a cross that Chicago bears very well, and its native residents wouldn't have it any other way.

Beginnings

Though Chicago was discovered in 1673 by Jacques Marquette and Louis Joliet as they were on their way to the Mississippi River, its first documented resident—Jean Baptiste Point DuSable—didn't "move in" until 1779. Monumental in United States history, the 1795 signing of the Treaty of Greenville provided that the Native Americans release the land on which much of modern-day Ohio, Detroit, and Chicago are located in exchange for payments (in the form of goods) as well as the continued permission for Native American people to hunt throughout the area. Construction on Ft. Dearborn commenced a few years later.

By 1808, American soldiers and their families were living within the walls of Ft. Dearborn (Markers indicating the exact location of

Ft. Dearborn can be found embedded in the sidewalks on the corner of Michigan Avenue and Wacker Drive). During the War of 1812, Commanding Officer General William Hull ordered Captain Nathan Heald to evacuate Ft. Dearborn and destroy all of the fort's excess arms, ammunition, and whiskey, while delivering the remaining goods to area Native Americans in order to mollify them. That plan failed, and the group of soldiers, militia, and their families attempted to escape to Fort Wayne, Indiana. Most of them were killed and the rest were taken as prisoners by a group of Native Americans that was 500 strong. That group went on to raze Ft. Dearborn, which was not rebuilt until 1816.

Over the next fifty-five years, Chicago grew by leaps and bounds, changing from a frontier village to a bustling center of activity. It became incorporated as a town in 1833, and then in 1837, a city. Its first mayor, William Butler Ogden, was elected. The Board of Trade was founded in 1848, and the first municipal structure was built that same year to accommodate the phenomenal growth that was taking place. The arrival of the telegraph connected Chicago to the West.

The 1850s brought the creation of the police department as well as the Chicago Historical Society. Major municipal structure changes took place; for example, many streets were raised by four to five feet—and as much as eight feet in some places—to accommodate for the sewer system and to facilitate drainage. Although the idea was mind-boggling to most people, many buildings were also raised, along with the streets, to the higher grade. These were amazing technological feats during that time.

Other gigantic leaps in innovation were also taken in the 1860's. Even after much of the city was raised, sewage still made its way to the lake, which caused fear of disease to spread rapidly. Starting at the shore and located sixty feet under the lake, a two-mile tunnel leading to a new intake crib was constructed as a solution. Clean water was also brought back to the city. A few years later, tunnels were constructed under the Chicago River as a remedy to the problem of stalled street traffic due to the opening of bridges that allowed tall vessels to pass through. These tunnels served vehicles and pedestrians at first, and much later were used by cable cars. As it happened, the tunnels became valuable escape routes during what is arguably the most famous Chicago tragedy—the Great Fire of 1871.

October 8, 1871 was a horrible day in Chicago history. A fire broke out in the barn behind the West Side home of Patrick and Catherine O'Leary located at 558 West DeKoven Street. The actual cause of the fire has been disputed over the years; the most popular theory is that Mrs. O'Leary's cow kicked over a lantern that started the blaze. How it began is less important than the damage it did. The fire completely razed the downtown area, and even jumped over the Chicago River twice to continue on its path. The casualty numbers are staggering: three hundred people died, 90,000 lost their homes, 17,500 buildings were destroyed, and the cost of all the damage was estimated near $200 million. (Someone still had a sense of humor, apparently: the front page of the *Chicago Tribunes'* first post-fire edition—on October 11—carried the headline *"CHEER UP"!*) The Water Tower is one of only a handful of buildings that survived the Great Fire of 1871. Today, the Chicago Fire Academy is located on the land where the O'Leary farm used to be.

With help in the form of food, clothing, and monetary donations from across the nation, the city rebuilt quickly and even expanded its boundaries in the process. The fire gave the city of Chicago a rebirth of sorts, allowing a fresh start in every area. Incredibly, the most obvious effects of the fire were gone within one year.

The Great Railroad Strike of 1877 was the first time that workers nationwide rose up in protest, and Chicago workers found themselves in the middle of it in July of that year. The Baltimore & Ohio Railroad levied a ten percent wage cut for their employees, and workers in West Virginia walked off the job in disagreement. Similar strikes in protest of wage reductions and other cutbacks spread to the West and eventually involved Chicago workers. Clashes between workers on strike and the police became ugly. Eventually, six companies of

U.S. Army infantry were brought in to put a stop to the violence and restore quiet.

As a result of the intense labor disputes of the railroad workers, George M. Pullman, inventor of the Pullman sleeper railroad car (as well as one of the men behind the raising of Chicago's buildings, years before), decided to build a model industrial town for his workers. He named the town after himself and wanted to create an environment that was far better than that which was available to workers elsewhere, resulting in—*he hoped*—less strikes and higher productivity levels. Construction on the town began in 1880 and was complete only four years later.

All of the buildings in the town of Pullman were made from brick. The Arcade building, which was a civic center of sorts, contained a bank, post office, library, theater, restaurant, and many shops. A hotel and one church were nearby. Parks and open spaces were plentiful, and the more than 1,000 homes had indoor plumbing, front and back yards, and maintenance and garbage pickup services that were included in the rent. Pullman ruled this perfect little town with an iron fist; he didn't allow outside newspapers, public speeches, town meetings, or alcohol consumption by town residents. He made all decisions regarding which shops could be established, which performances could appear in the theater, and which denomination could worship in the church. There were no city government offices in the town of Pullman, with the exception of the post office. The town of Pullman received international attention, and between 1881–94 won awards such as "World's Most Perfect Town." Problems would arise later, but for years, Pullman grew and thrived.

Chicago's transformation into a manufacturing center occurred throughout the 1880s as factories were constructed along the river and railroad tracks. Other parts of the city were growing, too. State Street became known for fantastic shopping in the department stores built by Marshall Field and Montgomery Ward. Taverns and vaudeville houses began to appear south of the shopping area on State Street, and Randolph Street became the home of the theater district. Jewelers centered their businesses at Wabash Avenue and Madison Street, and banks sprung up on LaSalle Street.

On May 1, 1886, union activists in Chicago supported the national movement for an eight-hour day by calling a one-day general strike. The strike at the McCormick Reaper Works factory on May third resulted in several deaths when unarmed workers clashed with the police. A rally of workmen was scheduled the following day near Hay-market Square. As police came on the scene to disperse the unruly crowd, a bomb was thrown (by a still unknown-assailant) into their ranks, and the police commenced firing into the throng of people. Many police officers and civilians were killed in the clash as the workmen returned fire. Eight men who were connected in some way to the riot and the radical organizations related to it were arrested and charged in the murder of the bombing victims. The jury ruled that all eight were guilty. One man was sentenced to fifteen years in prison, while the remaining seven were sentenced to death; four of these men were hanged, two of them had their death sentence commuted to life in prison, and one committed suicide. Governor John P. Altgeld even-tually granted a full pardon, but the Haymarket Affair remains one of the most horrific cases of misplaced justice in United States history. The martyrs of the Haymarket Affair have since been remembered on May first, International Workers' Day. The fight for the eight-hour workday was finally won in 1890.

The town of Pullman, which was once perfect, prosperous, and a major tourist attraction at the World's Columbian Exposition of 1893, was a victim of the depression of 1893-94 due to the failings of many railroad companies that were followed by a series of bank collapses. As Pullman's business profits started to decline, he made the decision to cut wages and increase hours for his workers but didn't lower the cost of living. This move was the final straw. People were angry. When Pullman would not discuss the poor conditions he was forcing on his workers and town residents, ninety percent of them went on strike. Eventually the town was annexed by the City of Chicago and later became a national landmark.

The World's Columbian Exposition and the Burnham Plan of Chicago

Experts credit two important events in history as being responsible for the transformation of Chicago into the world-class city it is today: the World's Columbian Exposition of 1893 and the Burnham Plan of Chicago. Both of these events not only shared a main contributor in architect Daniel Burnham and were major projects involving countless supporters of capital and creativity alike, but they also put Chicago on the international stage.

The World's Columbian Exposition was conceptualized as an 1892 celebration of the 400th anniversary of Christopher Columbus' voyage to the New World. The cities of St. Louis, New York, Washington, D.C., and Chicago competed fiercely for the privilege of hosting the World's Fair and representing the United States to the rest of the world. After it was revealed that the decision would be made according to which city had the deepest pockets, it all came down to New York and Chicago. Though New York looked as if it would get the honor, Chicago sailed in under the radar and won by raising millions of dollars overnight in an effort spearheaded by banker Lymon Gage. This response to the final offer made by the city of New York, adding to the dowry already established by notable Chicago citizens including Marshall Field, George Pullman, Cyrus McCormick, Philip Armour, and tens of thousands of "regular" Chicagoans who contributed in the form of stock subscriptions, put Chicago over the top.

Though opening day had been pushed back to 1893 (401 years after Columbus discovered the New World), there was no time to waste. After securing the services of architect Daniel Burnham and George R. Davis to spearhead this enormous construction project as the Director of Works and the Director General, respectively, the next step was to choose a site. After much consternation it was decided that Jackson Park would be perfect after the area was partially renovated. The marshy park had to be transformed into a miniature city by building up the ground in some places and adding streets, landscaping features like grass, flowers, and trees, lagoons, bridges, buildings, and more. In the end, the exposition site was made up of Jackson Park and the Midway Plaisance, which was a separate amusement area built to keep the noise generated by the attractions from disturbing the more peaceful park atmosphere where the buildings were located.

The design of the main grounds was under the direction of Frederick Law Olmsted, a prominent American landscape architect. Olmsted and his partner, Harry Codman, proposed an unconventional seascape design that would make use of the lakeside location and incorporate artificial pools and canals throughout the park. The buildings would be constructed on raised terraces.

Burnham gathered together a who's who of artists and architects to fill the exposition grounds with sculpture and Beaux-Arts style buildings. The buildings were covered with stucco and painted white, which caused visitors to refer to the area as the "White City." (The Palace of Fine Arts was the only "White City" building to have a brick substructure under its plaster façade and still stands today, housing the Museum of Science and Industry.) Exhibitions on display inside the buildings featured technology (Whitney's cotton gin, sewing machines), strides in agriculture (weather stations, farm-building models, and animals, of course), new products (Juicy Fruit gum, Shredded Wheat, Aunt Jemima syrup), goods (Tiffany & Co. jewelry, Remington typewriters), and much more. The sheer size of the exhibition halls was shocking to visitors, and the vast amount of offerings helped to make the exposition a huge financial and cultural success.

Most notable among the attractions, concessions, and sideshows along the mile-long Midway Plaisance was the very first Ferris wheel. Invented by George Ferris, an engineer who specialized in building steel frameworks for tunnels and bridges, the Ferris wheel was intended to be the showpiece of the World's Columbian Exhibition, much like the Eiffel Tower was for the 1889 Paris Exhibition. This gigantic "observation wheel," which made two revolutions per ride and cost fifty cents per person (the same cost as admission to the fair itself), housed thirty-six cars that could carry up to sixty passengers each.

The wheel proved to have a long-lasting impression on the more than 1.5 million visitors who enjoyed it as well as the city of Chicago itself. As a result of its popularity, homage to Ferris' original creation was built as the centerpiece of the newly renovated Navy Pier one hundred years later.

The Midway Plaisance also hosted ethnographic exhibits from the world over that were meant to introduce the general public to foreign cultures and different ways of life, including an African village and Streets of Cairo exhibit. Like the Ferris Wheel, these attractions came at an extra cost to visitors and exposed them to people and artifacts they never would have seen otherwise, since this was many years before television broadcasting came into play. The anthropological exhibits on the Midway were exhibited in 1894 after the Exposition in the former Palace of Fine Arts—now called the Field Museum of Natural History. The Field Museum was later relocated to the area now known as Museum Campus, and the Palace of Fine Arts was retooled to become the Museum of Science and Industry.

The World's Columbian Exposition gave city leaders a good idea of where Chicago fit in the world as well as a sense of optimism for the future. It left a legacy unparalleled by most other world's fairs. Globally, it impacted the areas of technology, business, consumerism, design, and culture in too many ways to list. The local impact was just as profound, perhaps most notably regarding its leading to the rise of the City Beautiful movement in Chicago. Daniel Burnham and the other proponents of the movement believed that the decay and demoralization of urban areas could be rectified with city planning that included wide streets, elaborate landscaping, and opulent buildings. The White City was just a small example of what was in store for the city as a whole.

Indeed, the city of Chicago needed some sort of plan. Between the years of 1830 and 1890, the population grew from 4,470 to more than one million inhabitants and grew to two million by the year 1910. Burnham believed that reorganizing the city in a piecemeal manner wouldn't work as well as starting from scratch with a citywide plan. He believed that employing the philosophies of the City Beautiful plan in Chicago would actually help the city run better because an attractive city would not only function more effectively than a dirty, unorganized one, but also be a more desirable place in which its wealthy residents would stay and spend their money. Burnham cited Paris, France as a model city to emulate, and he set out to gather moral and financial support for the complete renovation of Chicago.

Refusing to take a salary for his time and hard work, Burnham carefully developed a detailed plan — with, it must be noted, co-author Edward Bennett — that would combine beauty and utility for the betterment of the city. His research included the gathering of statistics, measurements, and other data related to the economic, social, and cultural life of Chicago, as well as building height measurements and detailed photographs of Paris. What he created for Chicago was right in line with the words Burnham is credited countless times with saying even though there is no firm documentation to prove it: "Make no little plans; they have no magic to stir men's blood and probably themselves will not be realized. Make big plans, aim high in hope and work."

Burnham found the backing he was looking for in the members of two prestigious organizations that merged in 1907: the Merchants Club and the Commercial Club of Chicago, whose mission was (and still is, according to the webpage that outlines its purpose and history at www.commercialclubchicago.org) to "promote the social and economic vitality of the metropolitan area of Chicago." Active members in the early 1900's included familiar faces such as Field, Pullman, McCormick, and Armour, plus Frederic Delano, Sewell Avery, Rufus C. Dawes, Charles H. Wacker, and Julius Rosenwald. The group promoted and underwrote Burnham's ambitious strategy for Chicago's renaissance, which was released on July 4, 1909 and presented in a spectacular, dark green, hardcover-bound, limited-edition book made up of 124 cream-colored pages that were gilded on the top edge and rough-trimmed on the side edge. The elaborate presentation was a way to further drive home the ideas contained inside. Such a grand book would surely, according to the Commercial Club (whose cipher was on the front of it), make the reader who was lucky enough to have a copy feel strongly about what was inside it. The text inside, detailing every aspect of the plan, was just as impactful on the readers as the included drawings and watercolors by Jules Guerin, black and white sketches by Jules Janin, and maps by the Plan's co-author, Edward Bennett.

The six major elements of Burnham's Plan of Chicago, which made provisions for the entire metropolitan area, included:

- Improving the lakefront
- Developing a highway system outside the city
- Improving the freight and passenger railway systems
- Acquisition of an outer park system
- Arranging systematic streets
- Creation of a civic center of cultural institutions and government

The improvement of the lakefront included adding parks (specifically, Grant Park) and a shoreline parkway. Burnham believed that landscaped parks not only beautified the city but also gave its residents a nearby escape from the stress of their daily lives. The highways were to be created in concentric circles extending from Wisconsin to Indiana. Trains, tunnels, subways, and an elevated transit system were to be built and located in areas of town that would be convenient and efficient for passengers and freight alike. The Outer Belt Park Commission, now the Forest Preserve District of Cook County, sought to establish a regional network of parks along the shores of Lake Michigan and outside the city. Burnham recognized that some of the busier city streets needed to be widened and new streets needed to be diagonally cut into the grid in order to make it easier for citizens to get around. The Field Museum's new (and current) building and government buildings near the intersection of Congress Parkway and Halsted Street were all part of the last element in the plan. Burnham's crown jewel, a tall, domed structure that would be the Civic Center, was meant to be the centerpiece of the city but never came to fruition.

Even with the support of some of the wealthiest and most respected men in the city, Burnham realized that a vital key to the success of the plan would be the support of the community as a whole. The hiring of Walter L. Moody to be the leader of the publicity campaign was an important step in the process. Moody created a more concise version of Burnham's Plan called *Wacker's Manual of the Plan of Chicago*, in addition to countless other publications. Moody and the Chairman of the Chicago Plan Commission, Charles Wacker, gave speeches to countless business people, civic groups, and government leaders in order to promote the plan and excite the public about the city's potential.

Moody involved Chicago's youth by convincing the Board of Education to include *Wacker's Manual* in the eighth grade civics curriculum. Eighth graders were targeted for several reasons: they were old enough to understand the plan and young enough to be impressionable, as well as the fact that many children quit school after the eighth grade, so this audience would be a larger one than the older grades. Moody had a long range of vision and realized that, if he could disseminate the information about the plan in the Chicago schools, the city's children might be able to go home and educate their parents about it.

Of course, like any major civic project that involves high finance and the approval of many people in authoritative positions, the Plan of Chicago wasn't completed to every exact specification, but its role in redesigning Chicago was major and has been felt ever since.

20th Century Growth and Suburban Sprawl

The city saw continued growth in the two decades that followed the release of Burnham's Plan. The City Council passed the Lakefront Ordinance in 1919, which caused the Illinois Central Railroad to situate their tracks below the grade of Michigan Avenue as well as use electricity for commuter trains. These changes enhanced the look and desirability of the area off of South Michigan, near Grant Park. The Roaring 20s were prosperous, and skyscrapers in the Beaux-Arts style sprang up, along with many new hotels, including the Palmer House

Hilton. The Wrigley Building, on Michigan Avenue at the Chicago River, was completed in 1924. Across the street, the Tribune Tower, a Gothic structure complete with flying buttresses and inset with stones collected by journalists from famous monuments around the world, was built in 1925. One of Chicago's great icons, Buckingham Fountain, was installed in Grant Park two years later. Enhancing river navigation during this time was the pioneering of the bascule (or rolling-lift) bridge, which splits evenly in half as it opens. Each weighted end acts like a seesaw when released. These bridges are among Chicago's most recognizable features today.

Chicago was affected deeply by the Great Depression. Many businesses closed their doors and peddlers combed the streets, looking for goods to sell. As shopping for luxury items came to a halt, stores began to shift their available merchandise to necessary items. The Work Projects Administration (WPA) was established in the mid-thirties by the federal government, providing jobs to many out-of-work Chicagoans. Lake Shore Drive and the State Street subway were two major projects built during this time, easing traffic congestion in the downtown area.

Because of its accessible location, Chicago became an important hub for transportation during World War II. Navy Pier was leased to the U.S. Navy at this time. More than 60,000 sailors and 15,000 pilots used the USS Wolverine and USS Sable (aircraft carriers which had been converted and docked at the pier) for training purposes. In 1947, the Chicago Transit Authority (CTA) was formed. The purpose of the CTA was to purchase and operate the city's mass transit (street-level railway, buses, and elevated train lines) within the same organization.

In the 1950s, new skyscraper designs in Chicago were a departure from the decorative, ornate style that had been customary and instead reflected the clean, modern style of the day. By the mid 1960's, older buildings were destroyed to make room for new ones made mostly of steel, concrete, and glass. City shopping boomed during this period. North Michigan Avenue became the trendier, high-end shopping destination as many stores moved out of the Loop area.

The Civil Rights movement of the 1960s, coupled with increased racial tensions downtown, led to riots on the West Side after the assassination of Martin Luther King Jr. Just a few months later, an anti-war protest in Grant Park during the Democratic National Convention became violent. The inner city was now, for many people, something to be afraid of, and growth slowed immensely for a long time.

Chicago became the center of attention once again in 1974, when the Sears Tower opened for business, four years after construction began. The building's design consisted of nine clustered "tubes" that varied in height beyond the fifty-story base. Sears Tower stood 1,450 feet tall (to the roof) when construction was complete, and was the world's tallest building until 1996 (The height of the building today, including the antennas that are not part of the original design, is 1,730 feet).

Starting in the 1980s, the powers-that-be in the city of Chicago began an intensive rejuvenation campaign in an attempt to bring people back to the downtown area. The goal was to ease fears about the city and lure visitors in to spend their money at hotels, stores, and restaurants there. Older buildings were repurposed; for example, the Chicago Public Library building became the Chicago Cultural Center. The exteriors and interiors of a few of the more prominent buildings were cleaned up and restored. The National Historic Preservation Act of 1966 and the Commission on Chicago Landmarks protected buildings of architectural and historical significance in the Loop area. The Pedway, one of Chicago's underground secrets, was built below street level to be used in any kind of weather as a retail space and network between buildings from City Hall to the Prudential Building.

Mayor Richard M. Daley was elected in 1989, and he immediately went to work on giving a facelift to Chicago as viewed by outsiders. Putting an emphasis on the attraction of tourism and convention business to Chicago, he backed many improvements in downtown development, which included further building renovations as well as street improvements. During his time in office, many of the high-rise buildings used for low-income public housing were destroyed in favor of the creation of neighborhoods filled with residents of mixed incomes and backgrounds. Navy Pier was made over and became the top tourist attraction in Chicago. Another popular destination, Museum Campus—home to the Adler Planetarium, the Shedd Aquarium, and the Field Museum—was created during Daley's tenure as well. Recently he played a major part in the creation of Millennium Park and Chicago's bid to host the 2016 Olympics (the honor went to Rio de Janeiro), and, with the help of the Mayor's Bicycle Advisory Council's Bike 2015 Plan, he sought to turn Chicago into one of the most bicycle-friendly cities in the United States.

The turn of the 21st century brought a new wave of residential development in the city, especially in the Loop. Hi-rise condos throughout the area (including those found in the brand-new Trump International Hotel & Tower) were a new, exciting draw for people who wanted to experience city living. Though the city continues to offer opportunities to live, work, and play, the suburbs have been through their own growth spurt.

Due to the crowding in the city and the lack of appreciable land, the middle class began to build houses beyond city limits in the 1950s, but there were many other factors that led to the development of the outer parts of Chicagoland. Corporations were leaving the city in favor of more space and offered higher salaries to workers who resettled their families outside of the city and in closer proximity to work. The highway system around the city, originally proposed in Burnham's plan, was constructed, starting with the Bishop Ford Freeway in 1956 and ending with the Stevenson Expressway in 1966. These major roads brought automobile travel and commuting to the forefront and made the developing suburban areas more car-dependent rather than railway-dependent. Shopping centers were built in the suburbs to accommodate residents so they could avoid traveling all the way to the downtown area.

Like the city, the suburbs saw continued growth at the end of the 20th century and the beginning of the 21st century. In 2005, five of the nine largest Illinois cities (behind number one, Chicago) were the suburbs of Aurora, Naperville, Joliet, Waukegan, and Cicero.

Many of the suburbs of Chicago have become internationally well known in their own right. For example, Naperville was placed near the top of *Money Magazine's* list of Best Places to Live in 2005, 2006, and 2008. Tinley Park was *Bloomberg Business Week's* "Best Place to Raise Your Kids" in 2010. Each town has a personality that is unique from any other.

Today's Chicagoland has something for everybody. A colorful history full of major catastrophes, battles, reconstructions, renewals, and harsh winters has given Chicago its strong image, and this leading city in the Midwestern United States continues to blaze the trails (no pun intended) of innovation on a worldwide stage.

Works Cited

Much of the information about the places in this book was culled from their own websites, which are listed in their respective sections. I used many other resources in writing the rest of the book, including the following great books and websites, which contain a vast amount of information about all facets of Chicagoland.

Bronsky, Eric and Samor, Neal. *Downtown Chicago in Transition*. Chicago: Chicago's Books Press, 2007.

Durkin Keating, Ann. *Chicago Neighborhoods and Suburbs: A Historical Guide*. Chicago: University of Chicago Press, 2008.

Heise, Kenan. *Chicago the Beautiful: A City Reborn*. Chicago: Bonus Books, Inc., 2001.

Hines, Thomas S. *Burnham of Chicago: Architect and Planner*. New York: Oxford University Press, 1974.

Home Page. City of Chicago's Official Tourism Site. 3 December 2010 <www.explorechicago.org>

Home Page. Historic Pullman Foundation. 24 June 2010 <http://www.pullmanil.org >

Home Page. Illinois Department of Transportation. 2 September 2010 <www.dot.il.gov>

Home Page. Chicago Southland Convention and Visitors Bureau. 3 December 2010 <www.visitchicagosouthland.com>

Home Page. The Burnham Plan Centennial. 14 May 2010 <http://burnhamplan100.uchicago.edu>

Home Page. The Commercial Club of Chicago. 22 June 2010 <http://www.commercialclubchicago.org/>

Home Page. The Illinois Tollway. 2 September 2010 <www.illinoistollway.com>

Home Page. The Local Tourist: Chicago's Neighborhood Website. 6 August 2010 <www.thelocaltourist.com>

Home Page. Woodfield Chicago Northwest Convention Bureau. 3 December 2010 <www.chicagonorthwest.com>

Interactive Map. WildOnions.org. 3 December 2010 <http://www.wild onions.org/InteractiveMap/NorthwestSuburbs_Chicago_Map.htm>

Inventor of the Week Archive. Lemelson-MIT Program. 7 July 2010 <http://web.mit.edu/invent/iow/ferris.html>

Kamin, Blair. *Why Architecture Matters: Lessons from Chicago*. Chicago: University of Chicago Press, 2001.

Mayer, Harold M. and Wade, Richard C. *Chicago: Growth of a Metropolis*. Chicago: University of Chicago Press, 1969.

McNulty, Elizabeth. *Chicago Then and Now*. Chicago: Thunder Bay Press, 2000.

Smith, Carl. *The Plan of Chicago: Daniel Burnham and the Remaking of the American City*. Chicago: University of Chicago Press, 2007.

The War of 1812. Galafilm. 15 June 2010 <http://www.galafilm.com/1812/e/events/ftdearborn.html>

World's Columbian Exposition. University of Virginia. 7 July 2010 <http://xroads.virginia.edu/~ma96/wce/title.html>

The verse that inspired the title of this book is a part of this fabulous collection, which was originally published in 1948:

Withers, Carl. *A Rocket In My Pocket: the Rhymes and Chants of Young Americans*. New York: Henry Holt and Company, 1988.

Index by Name

Index by Activity

Index by City

About the Author

Melisa Wells was born in Chicago and lived there until she was ten years old. She lived in Texas, Tennessee, Virginia, and Wisconsin before returning "home" sixteen years later, with her husband and two sons. She has been making up for lost time ever since.

Her first book, called *Remembering Ruby: For Families Living Beyond the Loss of a Pet*, was written for families with young children after the passing of her beagle, Bijoux, and the day it was published was one of her proudest. Melisa is also a freelance magazine writer, contributing feature articles about salon and spa management to *Nailpro* and *DAYSPA*. She has also written for *Chicago Parent: Going Places* and was a contributor to the book Hungry? Chicago Family (Hungry City Guides, 2006).

Melisa has blogged about parenting her teens at *Suburban Scrawl* since 2007, and is a contributing writer at two collaborative blogs, *The Chicago Moms* and *The Music Mamas*. She is active in social media, too. Find her on Twitter at @melisalw and on Facebook at www.facebook.com/chickeninthecar.

Though she lives in the western suburbs of Chicago with her family, Melisa makes time for city visits as much as possible, during which she does not stop grinning from ear to ear. Her husband believes she needs an intervention.

To learn more about Melisa go to www.melisawithones.com.

About the Artist

Dylan Wells has been creating computer graphics since he was in elementary school. Though he used to design in Microsoft Word, Microsoft Powerpoint, and even Paint, he is now using programs like Illustrator and Photoshop to create and manipulate images professionally and just for fun. He is a college student majoring in Graphic Design.

To order Mountain Girl Press titles, please go to
www.mountaingirlpress.com

Take a step back in time to the Civil War Era and enjoy a rich and compelling tale woven by Suzanne Mays in
The Man Inside the Mountain.

Essie Bell, is a woman alone on her farm in rural West Virginia during the last months of the Civil War. Mourning the death of her husband, and yearning for the son presumed dead by the Union Army, life could not be any harder. While everyone else urges her to sell her farm and move to town, Essie finds it a place a solace. When new people begin to enter Essie's life she finds she is still needed. If only she could answer the burning question, "Who is the man inside the mountain?"

Join author Tammy Robinson Smith for a literary treat for all ages,
Emmybeth Speaks.

Emmybeth Johnson is a nine year old girl who lives in Little Creek, Tennessee in the foothills of the Appalachian Mountains. Her story begins late in the summer of 1971. Emmybeth likes to know what is happening with the adults in her life and in the community in general. She has a favorite "hidey hole" where she can listen as her mother, grandmother and the ladies from her church's sewing circle discuss the latest news and gossip from Little Creek. Emmybeth treats the reader to the "goings on" of the community from her naïve perspective, which is sometimes closer to the truth than she knows!

Visit the hills and hollers of Kentucky as Susan Noe Harmon explores the lives of three generations of Appalachian women in her first novel,
Under the Weeping Willow.

Step into the lives of one Kentucky family who will capture your heart and leave you wanting more. Belle, Pearl and Sara, three generations of Appalachian women, will teach you about life in a 1950s family and how it touched the future. *Under the Weeping Willow* is a story about the closeness of family and how they enjoy the good times and pull together through the bad. Come into their world and live and learn from it along with them. You will feel like you've found a home and a family of Kentucky kin.

To read more about *Little Creek Books'* other titles please go to

www.littlecreekbooks.com

Nonfiction Titles

TO HIDE THE TRUTH, Susan Noe Harmon

SINKING CREEK JOURNAL: An environmental book of days, Fred Waage

EATING LOCAL IN VIRGINIA, Phyllis Wilson

IN THE GARDEN WITH BILLY: Lessons About Life, Love & Tomatoes, Renea Winchester

MOUNTAIN WISDOM: Mountain Folk, Judith V. Hensley

CHICKEN IN THE CAR AND THE CAR WON'T GO: Nearly 200 Ways to enjoy Chicagoland with Tweens and Teens, Melisa Wells

Young Adult Fiction Titles

MARTY MATTERS & MARTY MAYHEM, Jessica Hayworth

SARA JANE IS A PAIN, Rebecca Williams Spindler & Madelyn Spindler

Fiction

DEATHOSCOPE, John Clark, MD

THE TRAVELING TEA LADIES, Death in Dallas, Melanie O'Hara Salyers

Children's Books

WILLY THE SILLY-HAIRED SNOWMAN, Connie Clyburn

Poetry

HEART BALLADS: A potpourri of poetry, Betty Kossick

More . . .

Would you like to purchase extra copies of *Chicken in the Car and the Car Won't Go: Nearly 200 Ways To Enjoy Chicagoland With Tweens and Teens?*

Was your favorite Chicagoland attraction missing from this edition?

Do you want the scoop on author appearances?

Visit *www.chickeninthecar.com* for more information!

Become a fan of *Chicken in the Car and the Car Won't Go* on Facebook to get updates and bonus information in your news feed. Don't miss out on the Fun!

www.littlecreekbooks.com

CPSIA information can be obtained at www.ICGtesting.com

260955BV00001B/2/P